Repurposing the Green Belt in the 21st Century

Repurposing the Green Belt in the 21st Century

Peter Bishop
Alona Martinez Perez
Rob Roggema
Lesley Williams

UCLPRESS

First published in 2020 by
UCL Press
University College London
Gower Street
London WC1E 6BT

Available to download free: www.uclpress.co.uk

A CIP catalogue record for this book is available from The British Library.

ISBN: 978-1-78735-886-7 (Hbk)
ISBN: 978-1-78735-885-0 (Pbk)
ISBN: 978-1-78735-884-3 (PDF)
ISBN: 978-1-78735-887-4 (epub)
ISBN: 978-1-78735-888-1 (mobi)
DOI: https://doi.org/10.14324/111.9781787358843

There is perhaps no need of the poor of London which more prominently forces itself on the notice of anyone working among them than that of space. ... How can it best be given? And what is it precisely which should be given? I think we want four things. Places to sit in, places to play in, places to stroll in, and places to spend a day in.

Octavia Hill (1838–1912), founder of The National Trust

The Green Belt boundary cannot be drawn with perfect rationality. There is no clear divide between town and country on historical or geographical grounds. The only division we can see today is the one we have caused to be drawn on the map. It has, in a way, acquired the significance of its own history: just because we have once drawn the line, it has become part of the south-eastern structure.

Tomorrow's London – Background to the GLDP, *1974*

And yet, this 65 acres of exhaust-smudged scrub on the outskirts of St Albans has become the battleground for a clash between ambitious developers, who want to turn it into a care home, and a community who like things the way they are. The dispute is typical of the intractable discussions happening across Britain, as the population struggles to balance the need for development with a passion for rural preservation.

Ed Hammond commenting on a dispute regarding development in St Albans, Financial Times, *2012*

Contents

List of figures

List of tables

Acknowledgements

We are grateful to June Barnes, Richard Knox-Johnson, Nicholas Shrimpton, Richard Timmerman and Yuerong Zhang who generously helped the authors with their time and expertise. The content of the book does not necessarily reflect either their individual views or those of their organisation. Special thanks to Catherine Bradley for her copy-editing work on the text.

Introduction

Peter Bishop

The conflicting ideals of the urban and rural condition have been played out since classical times. The city has often been associated with problems of sedition, crime and disease, the home of a dangerous underclass. In contrast the countryside has been viewed by some as the 'natural' habitat for humankind, a lost Eden. It was, however, the advent of the industrial city that focused the attention of urban thinkers and reformers on the inter-relationship between city and countryside. The former might be a necessity, but it was also a place of darkness and grime, a seedbed of immorality. As the city spread outwards and 'contaminated' its surroundings, it was increasingly viewed as a beast to be contained.

Early concepts of planned and protected green areas around cities can be traced back (in their modern form) to the 1860 parkland towns of South Australia, Ebenezer Howard's Garden Cities and the Depression-era Green Belt towns of the USA. Green Belts[1] have since become a widespread instrument of urban planning in many countries around the world. Japan, Korea, the Netherlands, Germany and New Zealand are among many countries that have taken up the concept and tailored it to suit their own circumstances. Green Belts have become one of the most potent examples of 'branding' in town planning, recognisable to people who know relatively little about planning policy. The very name conjures up an image of a bucolic countryside that is hard to criticise.

The London Metropolitan Green Belt now covers 5,085 square kilometres and parts of 68 different districts or boroughs.[2] Originally it was a response to the outward growth of London and a fear that the countryside would be swamped by low-density suburbs and industry, that settlements outside London would be engulfed by the metropolis and that Londoners would lose access to the recreational and health benefits of the countryside. Latterly the Green Belt has become an area of contention between groups that want to preserve it at all costs and those that see the easing of restrictions as an easy answer to London's housing shortage. This is a conflict with deep roots in English attitudes towards the countryside.

The celebration of the virtues of the countryside has long been embedded in the English psyche, from the 18th-century Romantic poets such as Coleridge and Wordsworth to the landscape paintings of Constable and Turner and the writing of John Ruskin. The English industrial city may have been an economic necessity, but it was viewed with suspicion. The city was portrayed as a place of ill health and moral ambiguity: a bed of seething social and political unrest containing a dangerous underclass (Booth's 'vicious and semi-criminal' classes).[3] Such opinions led to the emergence of the urban reform movements around health, housing and parks (as well as abstinence). Alongside the celebration of the countryside came actions to preserve it and the creation of bodies such as the National Trust. From the 1890s campaigners were proposing the first early ideas of Green Belts around cities as places for recreation and solace for the urban population.

In this context the resonance with Ebenezer Howard's ideas – an idealised (sub)urban form of Garden Cities, each self-contained, surrounded by a *cordon sanitaire* of agricultural land and linked to each other by rapid transportation systems – is hardly surprising. At the heart of this thinking rests an ideal of the 'good life' centred on the family unit and where work and leisure might co-exist within well-defined zones. This socio-political ideal was as much moral as spatial. What is surprising is the durability of Howard's ideas. His spatial form is basically suburban and his populace middle class. The physical form of the few of Howard's Garden Cities that were built (Letchworth and Welwyn Garden City) is clearly recognisable in the ideals of 'Metroland', London's inter-war suburbs. The same ideas re-emerge in the post-war period with the New Town movements, from Harlow and Stevenage in the 1950s to Milton Keynes in the 1970s. Indeed, the spirit of Howard survives today, with the 2014 Wolfson Prize[4] competition for 40 new Garden Cities and numerous references by national politicians to 'Garden Cities' as the solution to the UK's housing shortage.

There are strong parallels between this nostalgia for the garden city and the desire to contain cities. Both entertain conservative views that are essentially anti-urban as well as a narrow spatial perspective of urban form that is to be contained within clear boundaries. When critically examined, however, the Green Belt, at least in the UK, is not the result of a rational planned process. Its present extent is rather due to a series of incremental decisions that stretch back over 100 years. The challenges facing cities in the 21st century are very different from those of the 19th and 20th centuries, yet the policy of protecting the countryside around cities from development has been surprisingly slow to evolve. In a time of rapid and potentially catastrophic climate change, the interrelationship of cities and their regions is far more complex (and inter-dependent) than before.

The Green Belt is now coming under increased scrutiny, however, particularly with regard to the shortages of affordable housing in London and the South East. The debate concerning Green Belt release is highly emotive. While there is general agreement that an acute housing shortage exists, particularly in London and the South East, there is disagreement over whether compact city models that focus on 'brownfield' land can provide sufficient developable land. The debate about the Green Belt should be far wider than the accommodation or limitation of the urban form.

Policy restrictions on the outward growth of cities create other urban issues. The current Green Belt debate largely ignores related questions such as the moves towards 'hyper-density' housing on limited brownfield sites, the changes to the London skyline, models of suburban densification and imperfections in the housing market. The urban region also represents opportunities to generate energy, grow food, clean and store water, recycle and reuse waste materials. Green Belts contribute to lower temperatures and mitigate heatwaves. They are fundamentally important in building urban resilience and can be a biodiverse ecosystem as well as places for recreation, exercise and enjoyment.

The rapid growth of cities around the world is placing a series of new and different pressures on their immediate hinterlands, particularly in the developing world. In many of these countries technical planning systems are often weak and can in any case be circumvented. This mirrors a condition that existed in the UK and Europe at the end of the 19th century. The urban periphery will vary from the shanty towns on steep hills around Caracas and Medellin to the sprawling, informal settlements and slums around cities such as Johannesburg, Mumbai and Lagos to the dormitory suburbs around Guangzhou and Shanghai. These peri-urban areas are frontiers and zones of transition – the yet to be consolidated city. However they are beginning to elicit particular policy responses, especially in China, where there are now moves to limit the outward sprawl of cities through the establishment of city limits and designated Green Belts. Yet such limitations on outward growth are rarely successful without some form of complementary policy that encourages urban renewal. Even where this exists, the urban edge might still be an area dominated by informal activities, horticulture, brick fields, waste dumps and low-grade industry. Designated city limits or Green Belts may be a well-tried policy response, but their application needs to be specific to the city concerned and its geographical, political and environmental context.

It is timely to revisit the theory and rationale for Green Belts and reflect on their changing roles from the time of their inception to the present day. Green Belts were originally intended 'to provide a reserve supply of public open spaces and of recreational areas and to establish a green belt or girdle of open space' (Greater London Planning Committee 1935). However, the concept changed in the immediate post-war period into a mechanism to limit urban growth (and in effect preserve the amenity of populations living outside the city limits). Meanwhile, pressing issues such as climate change, resource depletion, the relationship between the city and its natural environment and urban resilience have led to a more sophisticated debate about the city and its region: landscape urbanism. This debate is now raising fundamental questions about the purpose of the Green Belt in the 21st century.

In this book we will assess the history and rationale for the Green Belt. We will consider European and North American theories of urban planning that relate to urban edges and urban and rural spatial models. We will also examine methodologies for repurposing and restructuring the Green Belt through a series of case studies in London. Finally, we will reflect on ways in which Green Belt release (if, indeed, it is desirable) might take place within alternative legal and financial models; whether there might be methods for planned rationalisation of the urban edge; and whether the uplift of land values that occurs when open land is rezoned might be captured for wider social benefit.

This book has a particular emphasis on the UK, and especially on London. It is here that the ideas behind the Green Belt first crystallised and where the debate concerning its role and future is particularly topical. By examining the growth of the Green Belt and alternative models from other countries, it is hoped that a useful contribution to this debate might be made.

Notes

1. In 2017 there were 1,634,700 hectares of designated Green Belt in England, or 13 per cent of its total land area. Scotland has 11 designated Green Belt areas in the central area between Glasgow and Edinburgh, around Ayr, Aberdeen, Perth and St Andrews. Northern Ireland has 30 designated areas totalling some 22,600 hectares or 16 per cent of its land area. There is currently no designated Green Belt in Wales.

2. Ministry of Housing, Communities and Local Government (MHLG) 2019.
3. Booth 1889.
4. URBED 2014.

References

Booth, Charles. *Life and Labour of the People.* Vol. I, 1889; Vol. 2, 1891. London: Macmillan, 1902–3 (complete volumes).

Greater London Planning Committee. Town Planning Committee (1923–35) and Town Planning and Building Regulation Committee (1935–40). LCC/MIN/11,160, 1935. https://discovery.nationalarchives.gov.uk.

Ministry of Housing, Communities and Local Government. *Local Planning Authority Green Belt: England 2018/19.* Planning: Statistical Release, 18 October 2019. https://assets.publishing.service.gov.uk/government/uploads/system/uploads/attachment_data/file/856100/Green_Belt_Statistics_England_2018-19.pdf.

URBED. *Uxcester: Garden City*. Final Report: Wolfson Economics Prize 2014. http://urbed.coop/sites/default/files/20140815%20URBED%20Wolfson%20Stage%202_low%20res3.pdf.

Chapter 1

A lost Arcadia: the historical emergence of Green Belt thinking in the UK

Peter Bishop

The idealisation of the countryside and the evils of the city

Throughout history the relationship between the city and its countryside has exposed tensions. As far back as the first century BC, Cicero praised the virtues of '*civitas*' while Horace expressed nostalgia for the countryside: *Omitte mirari baetae fumum et opes strepitumque Romae*' ('do not admire the smoke and riches and din of blessed Rome').[1]

In the Renaissance the ideal of Arcadia was portrayed in art as the beautiful, secluded area where its inhabitants led simple, unsophisticated yet happy lives – in apparent contrast to the bustle and vice of the city. In the 18th century this ideal began to filter into England. An early idealisation of nature occurred in the great age of 18th-century landscape gardening. Following William Kent, Lancelot 'Capability' Brown (1715–83) perfected a form of 'gardenless' landscape, complete with undulating topography, lakes and clumps of trees, that was in stark contrast to the formal garden compositions of the 17th century. This may have been a form of English Arcadia, but it was essentially an imposition of a 'created' natural landscape. Such designs began to go out of fashion as the burgeoning Romantic movement sought the dramatic power of untamed nature.

The vision of the countryside as a form of Eden – a natural habitat for humankind to live in innocent harmony with nature – gained credence in the English Romantic movement. One of the main themes of Wordsworth and Coleridge's *Lyrical Ballads* (1798) was a return to the original state of nature, building on Rousseau's philosophy that humanity was essentially good but had been corrupted by the influence of society. This thinking occurred at a time of unprecedented change in English society. Between 1604 and 1914 5,200 Enclosure Acts were passed and 6.8 million acres of common or 'waste' land were removed from public access and use. Paradise, or at least Arcadia, was in decline. The Agricultural Revolution and the Enclosure Acts fundamentally altered the face of the countryside. They caused a drift to the cities and fuelled the beginnings of industrialisation.

Wordsworth and Coleridge were inspired by the Lake District, a seemingly wild natural landscape, and their ideas were in marked contrast to the ideals of control, rationality and order that underpinned the Enlightenment. This chimed with an erosion of traditional religious belief that relocated the notion of the divine into nature – later defined by T.E. Hulme as 'spilt religion'.[2]

The growth and rapid industrialisation of cities in the first part of the 19th century posed problems concerning the physical and moral health of these new 'citizens' and around governance (or at least the containment of potentially dangerous concentrations of poor people). The idea of a *cordon sanitaire* around cities was not new, however. As early as 1580 a proclamation of Elizabeth I (incorporated into an Act of Parliament in 1592) forbade the construction of 'any new buildings of any house or tenement within 3 miles from any of the gates of the said city of London'.[3] The proclamation was a response to the capital's growth, its increasingly unsanitary conditions and the need to provide food for a burgeoning urban population. In reality the motivation was principally a response to the influx into the city of labour that threatened to weaken the monopoly of the guilds. Although the result was the designation of a broad agricultural belt around the city walls, it was never systematically enforced. As with subsequent measures to protect the countryside and limit urban growth, it was not without a political agenda from powerful sectors of society.

What is perhaps noteworthy about Elizabeth I's proclamation was the fact that a form of urban sprawl was considered a significant enough problem to warrant legislation. In stark contrast to most other European cities, where warfare was still a constant threat, London was able to disregard the limits of a set of defensive walls and to grow outwards. In the 17th and 18th centuries the capital was on the cusp of rapid growth that saw it expand in a series of 'suburbs' – the Great Estates. New districts such as Mayfair and Belgravia were at the limits of horse and foot travel, but the advent of the railways enabled London to sprawl almost without limit. In contrast many other European cities still retained their defensive walls; these defined a border with the open countryside that lasted, in many cases, until the middle of the 19th century. The European city was more enclosed and compact, while London had already embarked on its journey towards suburbanisation.

London's new 'suburbs' became mainly the preserve of the fashionable and wealthy, with the poor largely confined to older inner areas and those surrounding the docks and industry of east London. The reaction against the problems of 19th-century urban life was understandable. Living conditions for the urban poor were often appalling, and many of the new industrial cities lacked any form of governance. Manchester, for example, was only incorporated as an administrative district in 1838, by which time its population exceeded 150,000. Edwin Chadwick's report in 1842 highlighted shocking statistics in Manchester, including a mortality rate of 57 per cent in children below the age of five and an average life expectancy of around 37 years of age.[4] Chadwick argued that it would cost less to provide decent housing than to support destitute families.

The condition of the 19th-century English city is well documented by writers such as Charles Dickens, reformers such as Charles Booth and commentators such as Friedrich Engels.[5] In 1865 John Ruskin described London as 'that great foul city of London – rattling, growling, smoking, stinking – a ghastly heap of fermenting brickwork, pouring out poison at every pore'.[6] Dickens' description of 'Coketown' (believed to be a fictitious version of Preston) both taps into a nostalgia for a more 'innocent' period and sums up contemporary perception of the 19th-century city:

> It was a town of red brick, or of brick that would have been red if the smoke and ashes had allowed it … tall chimneys out of which interminable serpents of smoke trailed themselves for ever and ever, and never got uncoiled. It had a black canal in it, and a river that ran purple with ill smelling dye, and vast piles of buildings full of windows where there was a rattling and trembling all day long, and where the piston of the steam engine worked monotonously up and down…[7]

The cholera epidemics of the 19th century (attributed by Dr John Snow in 1854 to a contaminated water supply) finally initiated the movements for urban reform and the birth of the modern town planning system. Exacerbating these problems in the growing metropolis was the impact of alcohol. The 18th-century gin craze had prompted John Wesley's proclamation against alcohol and the rise of teetotalism as a movement in the 1820s. But alcohol was seen as only one of the symptoms of a dissolute and potentially dangerous urban proletariat, the lower echelons of which were described in Booth's London poverty maps as 'the vicious and semi criminal classes'.[8] The stage was set for new models of living and these were provided by reformers such as the Quaker John Cadbury and the Congregationalist Titus Salt. Their model settlements were well planned, sanitary and based around the ideals of hard work, self-improvement and teetotalism.

Ruskin's *Seven Lamps of Architecture* (1849) set out a 'manifesto' for the Gothic Revival arguing that innovations, particularly from the Industrial Revolution, had subsumed the spiritual content and vitality of architecture. Underpinning his proposals were the ideals of craftsmanship, honesty in the use of materials, cultural memory and beauty inspired by nature. Influenced by Archibald Alison,[9] his thinking portrayed the countryside, rather than the city, as the 'natural' abode of humanity. In *Modern Painters* (1843–60) Ruskin references Wordsworth and his celebration of nature; similar ideas emerge again in *The Stones of Venice* (1851–3), which contrasts the dense urban form of medieval Venice with the wild nature of the lagoon, its boundary. His thinking influenced William Morris and the Arts and Crafts Movement, as well as a generation of social reformers.

The 19th century was an era of reform and philanthropy. The problems arising from poor urban living conditions, particularly their impact on public health, led to the Artisan Dwellings Act of 1875. This set basic standards for the design and spacing of new housing and empowered local authorities to clear slums and construct social housing. Octavia Hill, a friend of Ruskin, campaigned for improved housing conditions for the urban poor. She also recognised the importance of open spaces that were easily accessible to the urban population: 'the life-enhancing virtues of pure earth, clean air and blue sky'.[10] In 1883 she wrote:

> There is perhaps no need of the poor of London which more prominently forces itself on the notice of anyone working among them than that of space. ... How can it best be given? And what is it precisely which should be given? I think we want four things. Places to sit in, places to play in, places to stroll in, and places to spend a day in.[11]

Hill's legacy remains today in the form of Wimbledon Common, Hampstead Heath and Parliament Hill. Along with J.S. Mill, Canon

Rawnsley and William Morris, she was an early member of the Commons Preservation Society, whose actions in 1866 saw the removal of railings around Berkhamsted Common – an early example of direct action. The Society went on to merge with the National Footpath Society in 1899 and remains active today as the Open Spaces Society.

The National Trust, founded in 1895 and given statutory powers in 1907, was established with the express purpose of preserving important tracts of countryside and buildings through *acquisition* (either by gift or public subscription) and with the explicit objective of allowing public access. The Trust is now one of the largest private landowners in the country, responsible for 610,000 acres.[12] Other areas of open land were also being safeguarded. Epping Forest, for example, was purchased with the stated aim that it 'shall at all times keep Epping Forest unenclosed and unbuilt on as an open space for the recreation and enjoyment of the people'.[13] On the occasion of a royal visit in 1882, Queen Victoria declared 'It gives me the greatest satisfaction to dedicate this beautiful forest to the use and enjoyment of my people for all time'.[14]

These late 19th-century reform movements should be seen as part of a societal response to the problems of the city and the conditions of its inhabitants. Local government was in its infancy and the Victorian state was nothing like as extensive in scope as its modern counterpart. The reform movements were closely linked to acts of philanthropy that grew out of Non-conformism. The ideals of social justice were powerful drivers behind this movement and access to the benefits of the countryside were one aspect of this. This was entirely different from the idea of the countryside being protected in order to *limit* urban growth. The countryside surrounding cities was now seen as a resource for the enjoyment of urban populations, a belief that was to be the main driver behind the early attempts to create 'Green Belts'. Fears about the consequences of urban sprawl were at that time separate concerns.

The growth of the railways in the second half of the 19th century gave rise to the modern low-density suburb, where clean air and access to nature could be combined with access to work and entertainment in the city. New typologies of low-density housing led to the city's rapid outward spread. Although suburbs might overcome many of the perceived evils of the 19th-century city, they also gave rise to fears of the loss of countryside through urban sprawl. Indeed Ruskin raged against the impact of urbanisation when it reached Croxteth Lane in Dulwich.[15] However, the new and powerful institutions of local government were able to deliver improved housing, libraries, schools and municipal parks, and there was new interest in town planning, a profession separate from architecture and embedded in urban improvement. Social campaigners and thinkers sought new forms of settlements, places that espoused the social ideals of the family, hard work, proximity to nature and, of course, temperance.

The spirit of these new urban forms was famously set out by Ebenezer Howard (1850–1928). An enduring vision for 'utopian' living is epitomised in his 'Three Magnets' diagram that depicted pull factors from both towns and rural settlements leading to the creation of a vision of 'Garden Cities'.[16] These would-be settlements provided space where the benefits of town and countryside might co-exist. The 'ideal' city that Howard proposed would possess the following physical characteristics:

- Beauty of nature, social opportunity
- Fields and parks of easy access
- Low rents, high wages
- Low rates, plenty to do
- Low prices, no sweating
- Field for enterprise, flow of capital
- Pure air and water, good drainage
- Bright homes and gardens, no smoke, no slums

These characteristics suggested a clear physical division between industrial areas and residential districts, as demonstrated in the eventual construction of Letchworth. Howard's work, a radical response to the 19th-century city, was underpinned by the social ideals of 'freedom' and 'cooperation'. But it was different to the work of the social reformers who were concentrating on alleviating the conditions of the poor and destitute *within the confines of the city*. Howard seemed to accept that the Garden City was a utopian experiment when he suggested that his vision was only realisable by a pool of talented professionals with stakeholder interests in the built environment – architects, artists, medical men, experts in sanitation, landscape gardeners and so on. The Garden Cities movement resulted in a series of experimental suburbs including Bedford Park, Hampstead and Ealing Garden suburb. As London's population continued to grow, imitations emerged such as Merton Park in South London and Gidea Park in East London – both built during the first part of the 20th century. The good life that involved access to nature was reserved for the few, not the many.

There is no doubt that Howard's work was important. It was an innovative response to the prevailing urban conditions. The key reasoning behind his approach was decentralisation and polycentricity in order to alleviate traffic congestion and reduce journey times to city centres.[17]

He proposed a radial distribution of small cities around a larger central city, with each city separated by a form of proto-Green Belt. His concept is represented by the 'City Cluster' diagram (Fig. 1.1). Similar experiments occurred in Germany during the early 20th century with the establishment of Garden Cities separated by forests and open land.[18] Later in the UK Barry Parker experimented with Howard's concept when he created Wythenshawe, formerly in Cheshire and now in the City of Manchester. This Garden City was surrounded by a 415-hectare Green Belt, at the low density of housing then associated with a higher quality of life.

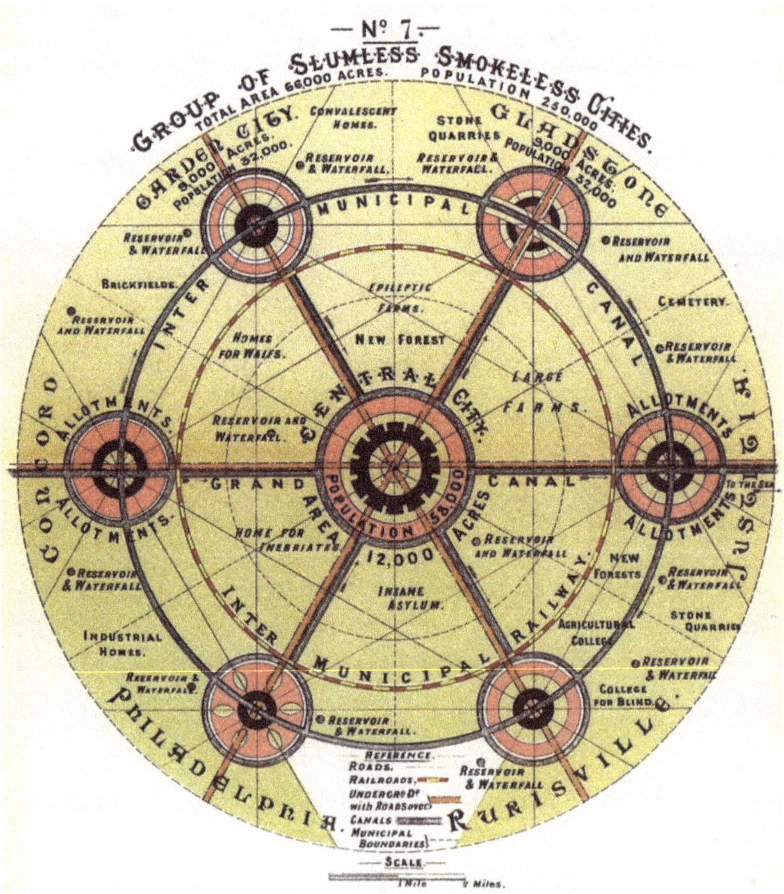

Fig. 1.1 Ebenezer Howard's 'City Cluster' diagram, 1902.

Source: Howard, Ebenezer. *To-Morrow: A peaceful path to real reform* (1898) and *Garden Cities of Tomorrow* (1902). London: S. Sonnenschein.

However, it is difficult to understand the enduring appeal of Howard's work today – well over a century later – when the urban condition is so different. The renewal programmes of the 20th century dealt with the deep-seated urban problems of the preceding century and gave urban populations access to open space for play and recreation. While decent housing and access to open space are still important, other issues such as social inequality, the exclusion of sectors of society from the opportunities of their neighbours, poor employment prospects, poor quality housing, disparities in health and life expectancy, obesity, air quality and sustainability are the new 'wicked issues' facing urban policy makers. These structural issues are centred in urban living and require urban-based solutions. In addition the UK is multicultural, at least in its urban centres. The idea of a small group of well-meaning individuals defining a general societal need and imposing a utopian rural/sub-urban solution on broad groups of society would seem ridiculous today. Or would it?

Apparently not. In 2014 the Wolfson Economics Prize was awarded for the design of a new Garden City and the Chancellor of the Exchequer, George Osborne, announced that the government would invest £300 million in 'the first proper' Garden City in Ebbsfleet, Kent. In June 2019 Lord Matthew Taylor told a conference on 'Building Sustainable Communities' that if each of England's rural local authorities built one new 5,000-home 'garden village' during the next decade it would deliver an additional one million desperately needed new homes. He suggested that this would answer the concerns of most residents as development would no longer be 'forced into their back yards'.[19] Perhaps this strange obsession with Garden Cities and the uncritical assumption that sub-urban living is a utopia may be explained by the power of branding. Garden Cities do have a resonance that New Towns lack. Furthermore, in the spirit of Thatcherism, their occupants would be mainly nuclear families and home owners.

The first Green Belts – for the urban or rural population?

While the utopian response sought a solution outside the realities of the city, a group of urban planners including Patrick Geddes combined urban geography, sociology and anthropology to analyse the urban condition. Their work focused on finding sensitive solutions through 'constructive surgery' rather than wholesale change through heroic deeds. Instead of trying to fit people into a theoretical model of a perfect society, Geddes placed the individual, and his or her needs, at the centre of his urban philosophy.

By the early 20th century London's expansion was causing increasing alarm. The growth of railway and road corridors presented a real possibility of conurbations merging along chains of linear development. Geddes combined his ideas of urban renewal with an interest in ecology and nature conservation, proposing 'Green Belts' to separate urban settlements. These ideas influenced Raymond Unwin's work in the 1930s, resulting in the establishment of London's first Green Belt. Howard had presented a simpler case for Green Belts as agricultural buffer zones around his Garden Cities. In his vision the surrounding countryside was largely functional; it would contain uses such as allotments, large farms and light industry, comprising a soft transition zone between urban land uses. Geddes saw the countryside in a broader context, a place for agriculture, certainly, but also a place for nature. This represents a significantly different approach to the conundrum of the city and its hinterland. Arguably it is his work that forms the foundation of more complex thinking about the city and its ecological region, ideas that are now being developed in the field of landscape urbanism (see chapter 4). Instead of considering open countryside as a barrier to urban growth, the interrelationship of city and countryside offers complex synergies. This relationship requires radically different approaches, particularly in the face of rapid and irreversible climate change.

The idea of enclosing urban areas with designated (and protected) countryside that was specifically for the enjoyment of their residents was not a new one – the earliest planned example is probably the Adelaide Park Lands of 1837. These Park Lands encompass both banks of the River Torrens and separate the City of Adelaide from Greater Metropolitan Adelaide, the capital of the state of South Australia. In continental Europe the issues associated with rapid urbanisation, slums, polluting industry, public health and transportation were common to most cities and urban planners were beginning to employ landscape strategies as a foil to the city. Broad boulevards were being used for urban renewal, from Haussmann's remodelling of Paris in the 1850s to the Ringstrasse in Vienna. The Ringstrasse, built between the 1860s and 1890s, was effectively a ring road, lined with grand buildings around the old city. Its form was determined by the path of the city walls that it replaced and its width imparted the dimensions of an urban park, separating the city centre from its suburbs. Beyond the Ringstrasse the city was free to expand (Fig. 1.2). In London, from 1890 onwards, various proposals had been put forward for some form of Green Belt around the city. One of the earliest came from

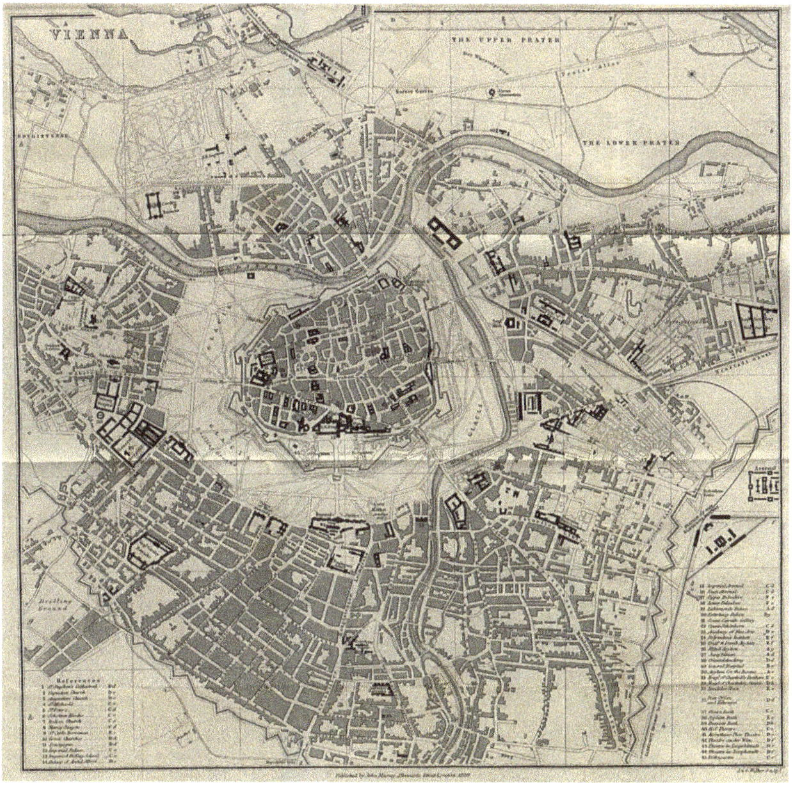

Fig. 1.2 Map of Vienna from *A Handbook for Travellers* (1858).

Source: A Handbook for Travellers in Southern Germany, 8th ed. London: John Murray, 1858.

Lord Meath (1841–1929), a Conservative politician who, together with his wife, was active in many charitable initiatives. He had been impressed by the broad boulevards of American cities such as Chicago and proposed a series of 'broad sylvan avenues' to connect open spaces in London. At the same time Meath also published proposals emphasising the amenity benefits of a 'Green Girdle' of variable size and depth. In 1901 William Bull MP published proposals for a half-mile wide 'Green Girdle' around London. In 1911 George Pepler proposed a strip of land around London that would also contain an orbital transport corridor at a cost of around £4.8 million – a huge sum for the time (Fig. 1.3).[20]

These ideas were far from the concept of a Green Belt. They were driven partly by transport requirements and partly by the idea of introducing a green ring for amenity use and allotments *into* the fabric of the

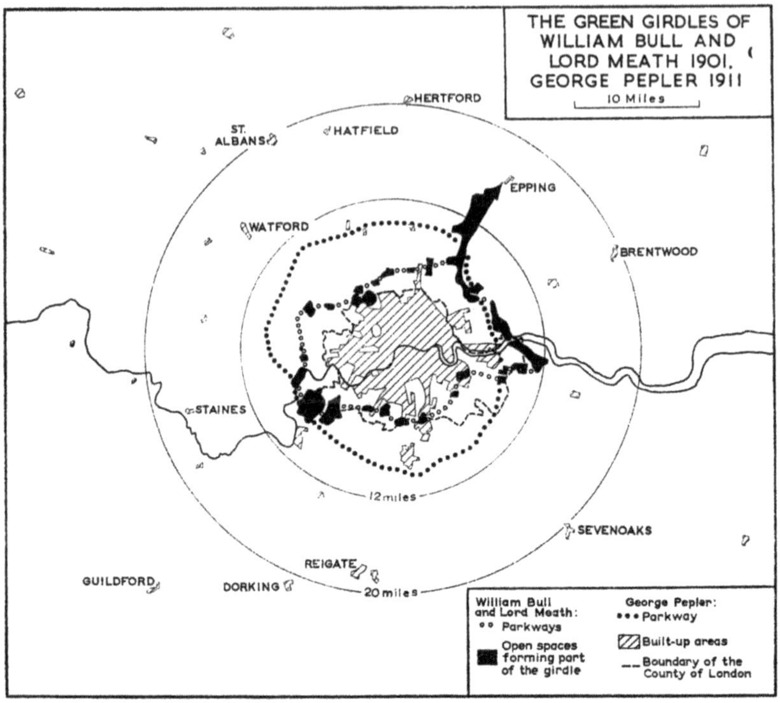

Fig. 1.3 Plan showing the 'Green Girdles' of William Bull and Lord Meath and of George Pepler, published in *The Sphere* (1901) and *Garden Cities and Town Planning* (1911).

Source: Thomas, D. 'London's Green Belt: The evolution of an idea', *The Geographical Journal* 129 (1) (1963): 14–24, esp. p.15.

city. As such, they were heavily influenced by Howard's models of Garden Cities. Attractive as they might have seemed, the ideas were devoid of any mechanism – political, administrative or financial – for implementation. This was partly rectified by the Housing and Town Planning Act 1909, which empowered local authorities to draw up land use plans. Dreams could now be legislated for, but without any form of metropolitan government they would remain dreams.

The idea of a Green Belt as it is meant today was proposed in 1919 by the London Society in its 'Development Plan of Greater London'. Together with the Campaign to Protect Rural England (CPRE), it proposed a continuous belt (of up to 2 miles wide) to prevent urban sprawl. Beyond this new development could occur. These proposals predated the modern town planning system which controls development through granting planning permission. Therefore the outward development of London was still effectively unregulated. Without any means of preventing development, the proposed solution was the public purchase of land.

The London Society saw the Green Belt as a largely agricultural zone. It proposed that land could be acquired and safeguarded using funding from agricultural rents. While this would bring land into public ownership, it did not address the growing issue of public access. Urban populations with spare income and leisure time were often prevented from accessing the open countryside by landowners. The mass trespass on Kinder Scout in 1932 illustrates this conflict. Around 700 ramblers walked by prearrangement onto this privately controlled moorland; in subsequent skirmishes with gamekeepers, six of them were arrested and jailed. The harshness of the sentences they received was widely condemned and a subsequent protest at Winnats Pass attracted around 10,000 people. Such conflicts highlighted the mounting problems of access to open space for urban populations.[21]

The relationship of the city to its countryside was stimulating debate across Europe. In 1913 the International Federation of Housing and Town Planning, founded by Ebenezer Howard, started to draw together standards of international best practice. In 1926 the International City Planning Conference considered ideas about regional decentralisation and the construction of satellite towns (with green space in between them). The London conference in 1935, attended by Raymond Unwin in his capacity as London County Council chief planner, discussed 'planned rural development and the preservation of the countryside'.[22] Some papers urged the preservation of the open countryside for recreation and food production in the face of advancing suburbanisation. German delegates presented alternatives to the centralised city in the form of agricultural settlements; these were based on the concept of *Heimat*, closely aligned to Nazi philosophy. They argued that this paradigm of rural life would alleviate overcrowded cities, provide employment and increase food production. In contrast the Italian architect Luigi Piccinato proposed to eliminate the distinction between urban and rural planning. He argued that planners should consider the town and the countryside as a single whole.[23]

The first Green Belt for London was formally proposed by the Greater London Regional Planning Committee (GLRPC) in 1935. The proposal stemmed from the work of Raymond Unwin, one of the instigators of Letchworth Garden City. In 1927 the GLRPC had been established with Unwin as its first technical adviser. Significantly the

GLRPC included the representatives from the London County Council (LCC) and authorities within a 25-mile radius of London. Although it had no statutory powers, there was for the first time a forum for strategic planning at a regional level. Unwin's first report (1929) proposed an agricultural buffer around London. By his second report (1933), Unwin's thinking had evolved to suggest a wider, although not continuous, belt of recreational and amenity land. This was influenced by a survey in 1933 revealing that in the absence of government powers or funding there had been an alarming loss of recreational land to development (8,500 acres) around London.

The 1932 Town and Country Planning Act had introduced some controls over the development of land. However, these were weak and did not provide a basis for the restriction of development through blanket zoning policies. In the absence of effective planning powers, the implementation of the Green Belt was down to purchasing land or using covenants that would restrict its development. The LCC Green Belt loan scheme was introduced in 1935. It allowed the LCC to provide loans to surrounding district councils to acquire land or negotiate covenants.

Table 1.1 shows the LCC contributions to such purchases between 1935 and 1961. The concept of government loans had already been established.[24] Between 1930 and 1934 the Ministry of Health had given loans to councils to purchase 1,455 acres of land. Some areas of Crown land, although restricted in theory to achieving 'best consideration', had also been designated as Green Belt, sometimes through a degree of subterfuge by civil servants who were sympathetic to the objectives of the Campaign to Protect Rural England (CPRE). Some used creative arguments

Table 1.1 Land purchased for Green Belt by public authorities (1935–61)

Area	LCC Contributions	Area safeguarded (acres)
Buckinghamshire	£101,849	5,059
Essex	£119,950	4,471
Hertfordshire	£189,111	4,138
Kent	£66,309	2,509
Middlesex	£294,459	5,915
Surrey	£156,129	3,754
Croydon	£36,019	594

Source: Amati, M. and Makoto, Y. 'The Establishment of the London Green Belt', *Journal of Planning History* 6 (4) (2007): 311–37.

to allocate land for military purposes or aerodromes, effectively preserving its open nature.[25] For example, the 380 acres of Fairlop Plain in north-east London was secured through designation as an aerodrome.

The stated purpose of the LCC-sponsored Act of 1935 was 'to provide a reserve supply of open spaces, not necessarily continuous, but as readily accessible from the completely urbanised area of London as possible'. The underlying objective was reformist and radical – to provide access to the countryside for the urban population. This is important and will be examined later in this chapter. The first Green Belt was seen as an integral part of London, providing space for the enjoyment of the population rather than a barrier to growth. The LCC offered to make grants available to purchase open land and pledged £2 million over the next three years for this purpose. Within 14 months some 18,300 acres had been purchased at a cost of £713,000. By 1938 a remarkable 68,000 acres of open countryside and agricultural land had been safeguarded. The Green Belt (London and Home Counties) Act 1938 enabled the LCC to consolidate its work on establishing the Green Belt. The Act severely restricted the erection of buildings on the Green Belt except where they were ancillary to the use of the land. It also required local authorities on London's extremities to define Green Belt areas on scaled maps and enabled local authorities to make bye-laws for the management of the land.

In the absence of any formal means of granting or refusing development, the only way of preserving it from development was to have a controlling interest. The Act granted powers for public bodies to *take ownership* of Green Belt land. This was cumbersome and expensive, but it did link the specific designation of Green Belt with beneficial use (agriculture) and public access (leisure and nature conservation). It should also be noted that in the post-Depression period land was relatively cheap. In 1926 the average price per acre was £30, but this price dropped further through the 1930s.[26] Today average prices range from £8,000 to £20,000 per acre. At the same time inheritance tax, first introduced at 15 per cent in 1894, rose to 40 per cent in 1919, 50 per cent in 1930 and 60 per cent in 1939. In such circumstances agreements to transfer land through bequests to public bodies were increasingly plausible. Finally, purchasing land for the enjoyment of all in perpetuity was very much in the spirit of the age, complementing the work of institutions such as the National Trust and moves to open up access to the countryside through footpaths and rights of way. Municipal authorities such as the LCC were powerful and interventionist. The idea of acquiring land for recreation was as much a part of urban planning programmes as buying land for new housing or roads.

Section 3 of the Green Belt (London and Home Counties) Act 1938 allowed local authorities and parish councils to acquire land by agreement, through compulsory purchase, as bequests or through entering into restrictive covenants with landowners. One of the stated uses of Green Belt land was camping – an activity that epitomised the spirit of opening up recreational use of the countryside. Land purchase continued through and after the Second World War. By 1944, in addition to land safeguarded through agreement and covenant, 25,000 acres had been purchased, with a further 1,126 acres bought by 1961 (Fig. 1.4). There was public access to 41 per cent of this land, the remainder being agricultural.

The policy of land purchase was remarkably successful. It was also politically popular. The needs of access to open countryside for

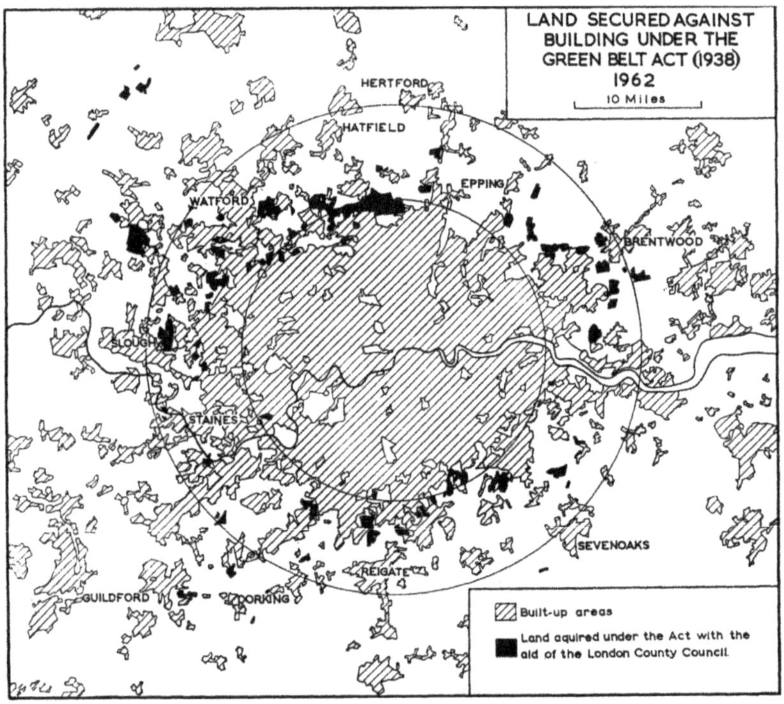

Fig. 1.4 Diagram showing land purchased by the London County Council under the Green Belt (London and Home Counties) Act 1938.

Source: Thomas, D. 'London's Green Belt: The evolution of an idea', *The Geographical Journal* 129 (1) (1963): 14–24, esp. p.15.

recreation might have been one of the driving factors, but it was the shires and district authorities that had to implement it. Their motivation was strong since their own populations comprised significant numbers of middle-class people who had opted to move out of London. They valued access to the countryside and the preservation of its open and rural character. By 1938 Essex, Middlesex and Surrey had safeguarded 42,200 acres of Green Belt.[27]

Local government was remarkably creative in securing land for Green Belt. As well as the outright purchase of land, the agreement of restrictive covenants and bequests, the weak planning powers from the 1932 Town and Country Planning Act were used creatively by some districts to trade development consents for areas of land that might be purchased at discounted rates or protected by covenant. This was an early example of 'planning gain'.[28] Another method was to threaten the compulsory purchase of land and then settle out of court. These trade-offs included agreements to 'sterilise' land from future development as well as covenants that allowed occupiers to enjoy the land during their lifetimes but to pass it to the district council thereafter. Some Crown land was designated for military uses, effectively preserving its open nature. Other districts acquired manorial rights dating back to the Norman Conquest. These were rights to use land without actually owning it, for activities such as hunting or grazing. Such manorial rights secured Upminster and Epsom Commons as Green Belt.[29]

The 1930s saw remarkable progress in securing a Green Belt based on preserving the countryside and enabling public access. There seems little doubt that this was a broadly popular movement driven by creative government for the public good. There was both a degree of altruism from some landowners in agreeing restrictive covenants due to a genuine desire to preserve the heritage of the countryside and a recognition that ultimately their own properties and estates would benefit if the rural setting could be preserved. Landowners might relinquish ownership, but not the control of amenity.

Limits to growth – post-war reconstruction

In the inter-war period the London conurbation grew rapidly. Sir Patrick Abercrombie's London Plan sought to address this by containing London's sprawl within a literal 'Green Belt' of undeveloped land. The first recognisable version of London's Green Belt appears in the County of London Plan (1943) that addressed five particular urban 'defects':

- Traffic congestion
- Depressed housing
- Inadequacy and the poor distribution of open space
- The mix of housing with industry
- Urban sprawl and suburbanisation

The ideas were developed further in Abercrombie's Greater London Plan of 1944 (Fig. 1.5), where four roughly concentric rings around London based on residential density and land use were proposed. The dense urban inner ring was surrounded by a lower density residential ring, surrounded in turn by a Green Belt. Beyond this was a fourth ring that contained agriculture and a series of New Towns. The Green Belt was to be anything from 1 mile to 6 miles wide (although Duncan Sandys MP argued that it should be up to 10 miles wide). The Green Belt was defined as 'a buffer between the expansion of London on the one hand and the regional communities along with farming on the other'.[30] Furthermore, the Green Belt was seen as both an agricultural zone and a continuation and completion of the urban park system. As such it was intended to meet both the agrarian and recreational needs of the London region.[31]

The Plan envisaged that the Green Belt would be connected by 'green wedges and parkways' to the central areas of London. It also stated that 'a good deal of this land which immediately adjoins the towns should be in full recreational use', although it went on to concede that the picturesque element of villages surrounded by productive agricultural land was, in itself, a pleasing element.[32] The emergence of agricultural land as a key component of the Green Belt reflected the wartime traumas that forced the cultivation of all available land to feed the population under the 'Dig for Victory' programme.[33]

In many ways Abercrombie's proposals for the Green Belt should be seen as a strategic concept rather than a specific set of proposals. There was no political entity beyond the LCC boundary (corresponding to today's central London boroughs) and therefore no authority with the remit or powers to implement it. The Plan also contained proposals for new orbital and radial roads and the Green Belt was one of the mechanisms to prevent the coalescence of settlements along transport corridors. Within London, the Plan proposed that all existing open spaces should be protected from development, that a variety of open spaces be established and that a series of parkways should be created to allow residents to walk between the major open spaces, unimpeded by traffic. The Lea Valley would become a regional park and other new parks would be created in areas of open space deficiency – generally the poorer

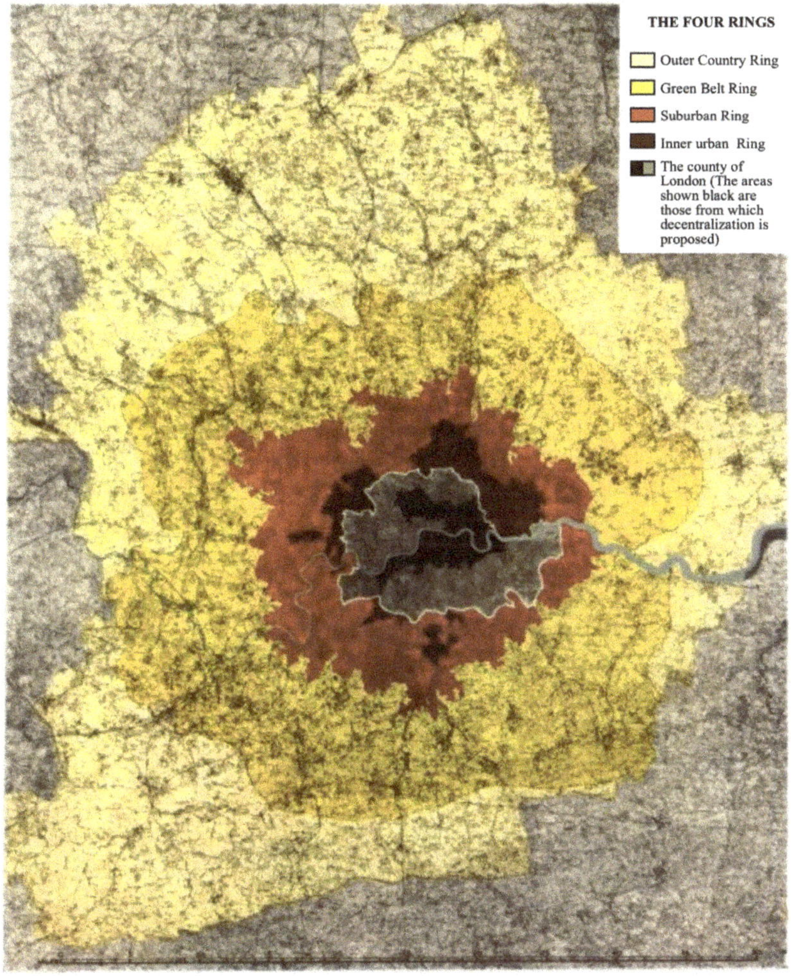

Fig. 1.5 Map of London's 1944 Green Belt (shown in dark yellow).

Source: Abercrombie, P. *Greater London Plan, 1944.* London: University of London Press, 1944.

neighbourhoods. These included Mile End Park in Tower Hamlets and Burgess Park in Southwark.

The Abercrombie Plan was light on implementation. This is not surprising at a time when the UK was on a war footing, with its economy centrally planned and largely controlled by the state. Abercrombie looked forward to post-war reconstruction where the state would be the major player in providing housing, infrastructure, schools and open space.

Although compared to today the state continued to be a major agent behind housing and social programmes, the weaknesses of the UK economy from the end of the 1940s until the 1970s meant that there were never sufficient resources available for planning on the scale that Abercrombie envisaged.

The introduction of the Town and Country Planning Acts of 1947 fundamentally changed the ways in which the Green Belt could be established and, consequently, the way in which it functions. That legacy, both good and bad, is with us today. Effectively the Town and Country Planning Acts removed unrestricted development rights from landowners. This form of confiscation or nationalisation was in keeping with the radical policies of the Attlee government that nationalised coal, steel and railways and set up a universal health and social welfare system. The right to enjoy one's property is, however, deeply embedded in the British psyche: it has been hard fought for and defended. Control over development rights was a radical but essential response to the complexities of economic life in the post-war period.

The Town and Country Planning Act 1947 required local authorities to produce development plans, a process that allowed open space – whether parks or open countryside – to be formally protected. It brought the obvious advantage that land purchase agreements were no longer required to safeguard land. This was particularly important in the post-war period when public funds were severely constrained and prioritised for reconstruction and the creation of the Welfare State. The downside, however, was that one of the key purposes of Green Belt, that of public access and enjoyment (*proactive policy*), became secondary to restrictions on development (*restrictive policy*). In other words, the Green Belt ceased to be seen as a resource for the active enjoyment of urban populations. Instead it became a zone that restricted development, arguably for the benefit of those who lived in it. This policy shift was significant but has largely been overlooked. It is revisited in chapter 3 which examines policy responses to the ongoing problems of urban growth.

The Green Belt enshrined

The consolidation of Green Belt policy that largely remains today was enshrined in Circular 42/55.[34] Underlying the Circular was 'the importance of checking the unrestricted sprawl of urban areas, and of safeguarding the surrounding countryside against further encroachment'. The Circular did not supersede the Green Belts Act 1938, but it did acknowledge the difficulties that local authorities faced when purchasing land for the Green Belt. Establishing control over development enabled authorities to take a completely different approach to the Green Belt – one that was considerably less costly and time consuming to implement. The Circular urged local authorities (wherever it is desirable) 'to check further growth of a large built-up area; prevent neighbouring towns from merging into one another and preserve the special character of a town'. It stipulated that Green Belts should be several miles wide in order to ensure 'an appreciable rural zone around all built-up areas'. It accepted a 'strictly limited amount of infilling or rounding off' of existing towns or villages, but specifically stated that in urban areas:

> every effort should be made to prevent further building for commercial purposes; since this, if allowed, would lead to the demand for more labour, which in turn would create the need for the development of additional land for housing. (!)[35]

The emphasis was clear. The outward growth of London and other cities was to be constrained. The Green Belt had become a spatial buffer zone. Open land was valued regardless of its value for public access or environmental issues. Residents of the rural areas affected quickly rallied to the cause. These rural hinterlands were mainly wealthy, Conservative-voting heartlands and were not to be touched. The justification was both a fear of the outward growth of the city and the pervasiveness of the paradigm of the English countryside. The desire to protect rural property values from erosion by an influx of the urban poor was rarely acknowledged, but is clearly in the shadows of this legislation. The urban poor were to be rehoused beyond the Green Belt in a series of New Towns. The basis of Circular 42/55 is essentially anti-urban. The evils of the city were to be contained, and planning policy allowed this to happen.

Contextually this policy needs to be seen against the specific needs of the period. Post-war reconstruction meant that new housing was required on an unprecedented scale and new light manufacturing industries needed efficient road networks and a skilled labour force. The ideals of planners such as Abercrombie were based on rational, modernist principles of the separation of land uses, zoning and efficient transport. The need to combat the ills of the pre-war period were evident in Abercrombie's enlightened thinking on open space, parks, schooling, health and lower density housing. The idea of rebuilding inner urban areas at the old densities was unthinkable. The model was for lower density suburbs – as characterised, for instance, by the rebuilding of

Canning Town's Keir Hardie Estate. The New Towns helped to reduce densities in central London and allowed for re-planning and renewal to provide much needed parks, school, roads and welfare facilities. All of these required additional open land either within an extended Green Belt (that was being designated at the same time) or beyond it. The ability to plan new settlements at the same time as creating a much larger Green Belt is a brief example in the UK of integrated spatial planning on a regional scale. In some ways this spatial dispersion of the city was the realisation of the ideas of Howard, rather than Geddes.

The regulation of urban sprawl was, of course, a welcome result of the Town and Country Planning Acts and the creation of Green Belts. The outbreak of the Second World War had largely halted suburban house building, freezing the urban edge. The subsequent designation of Green Belts – often very tightly drawn around the edge of existing settlements – did not result in a rational urban edge to cities such as London. Maps of the edge of London today show this clearly: streets enter the countryside like tendrils, only to be frozen in time. Suburban growth had never been planned to end as an incomplete project. Chapter 3 considers the implications of this in more detail.

Until the mid-1980s London's population was in decline, with growth occurring in the surrounding counties.[36] The implication of London's population decline was that any pressures for expansion into the Green Belt had been relieved. At the same time, between 1947 and the mid-1980s, the Green Belt around London expanded significantly and there is no doubt that the policy was popular. Attitudes towards the perceived failings of the early New Towns and overspill estates fuelled a move against further New Towns and urbanisation in general.[37] The policy was reappraised in the Clawson study of Green Belt restrictions in 1973.[38] Its main conclusions were:

- Containment. The amount of land converted from rural to urban uses has been minimised and also compacted
- Suburbanisation. A growing spatial separation of the new residential areas from the main employment centres
- The inflation of land and property values

This study demonstrated that the Green Belt might be working effectively according to the objectives of the 1955 Circular, inasmuch as it had contained sprawl, but that there were downsides as well. 'Suburbanisation' was occurring, with residential areas becoming separated from areas of work, particularly industry. This was significant since lower density suburban areas were likely to be more reliant on the private car. The construction of the M25 motorway, completed in 1986, was a response to this; it became almost immediately one of the busiest orbital roads in Europe, with some sections handling nearly 220,000 vehicle movements a day.[39] The second issue was the inflation of land values. The population of Greater London might be declining, but that of the South East was not. Encroachment on Green Belt land and greenfield sites was inevitable.

Despite the change in the rationale for Green Belt from recreational use to urban containment, a review of the London Plan in 1960 noted that while over 500 acres of new public open space had been created in the 16 boroughs under the LCC, in order to comply with the policy of 2.5 acres per thousand population, a further 2,258 acres were still required.[40] The Review reaffirmed the importance of the Green Belt noting that:

> the green belt scheme initiated by the Council in 1935 was… still very much alive. Planning powers alone do not secure public open space or extensive public access, and it is for these purposes that contributions have been made by the Council since 1947.

The 1960 Review contained no proposals to change Green Belt policy. The area remained very much the same as in previous plans (Fig. 1.6) and was still substantially outside the control of the LCC.

The London Government Act (1963) reformed London government, amalgamated smaller councils into larger units and created the Greater London Council (GLC). This new body covered all of the London metropolitan area, rather than just the inner conurbation, reflecting the realities and complexities of urban governance in the second half of the 20th century. For the first time a region that could be administered and planned as a single unit incorporated the inner fringes of the Green Belt. The boundaries of the GLC remain the same in the Greater London Authority (GLA) as reconstituted in 2000.

'Tomorrow's London' – a background document to the Greater London Development Plan (1969) – restated the importance of the Green Belt:[41]

> A little peripheral building, a belt a mile wide all the way around London … would give us enough housing. This argument fails to realise the cost to all of us … the main effect would be to choke our lines of communication … not only would travel to work become more difficult … but it would become equally more difficult for those living in the city to get out at weekends or holiday times.

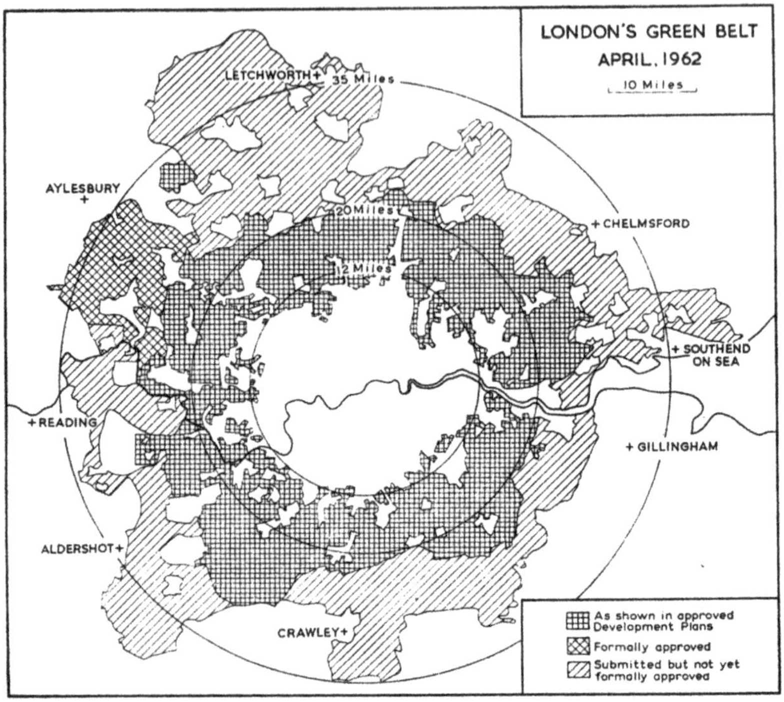

Fig. 1.6 Map of London's Green Belt from the Ministry of Housing and Local Government, April 1962.

Source: Thomas, D. 'London's Green Belt: The evolution of an idea', *The Geographical Journal* 129 (1) (1963): 14–24, esp. p.15.

In accepting the status quo, however irrational, the document rejected alternatives such as 'green wedges' or 'green setting'. In order to protect the concept of the Green Belt in its entirety more public access was proposed, as was the tidying up of derelict or waste land.

The Greater London Development Plan (GLDP) was published by the GLC in 1976. The Plan set out policies to retain the Green Belt as a mechanism to limit urban sprawl and as a place for recreation and agriculture. It also introduced a new category of Metropolitan Open Land (MOL). Metropolitan Open Land developed Abercrombie's policies for the protection of existing open spaces in London and provided:

> attractive breaks in the built-up area, relieving monotony of an otherwise continuous urban development … (these areas) are not appropriately situated for incorporation in the green belt, often

> forming islands embedded in the urban fabric ... They nevertheless need to be safeguarded just as much as green belt.

MOL was defined, as were appropriate uses:

- Public and private open space and playing fields
- Agriculture, woodland and orchards
- Golf courses
- Allotments and nursery gardens
- Cemeteries and crematoria

This move was important. In effect it introduced Green Belt policy restrictions to open land within the city itself. Over time the policy approaches to Green Belt and MOL became indistinguishable, the implications of which are considered in chapter 3. The GLDP was finally adopted in 1976. It expected local plans to define both Green Belt and MOL through zoning and policy restrictions, although the compulsory purchase of housing for urban parks continued into the 1980s before resources finally dried up.[42]

Notwithstanding the definitions in the GLDP (that only covered the GLC area) by the 1980s the Green Belt had become firmly established along the lines set out in Circular 42/55,[43] as a measure for the containment of urban growth. Circular 14/84 reaffirmed this:

> The Government continues to attach great importance to green belts which have a positive planning role in checking the unrestricted sprawl of urban areas, safeguarding the surrounding countryside from further encroachment and assisting in urban regeneration. [44]

In other words, the city was a threat to the countryside and its needs were subservient. However, the Circular does contain a subtle shift of emphasis on the debate with the first mention of the Green Belt having the effect of 'recycling derelict land for urban renewal'. Restrictions to outward growth had the advantage of concentrating investment back into existing urban areas. This was significant since London and other major cities in England were then emerging from a period of dramatic economic restructuring, leaving large swathes of derelict and contaminated land. These included the London docklands. In 1981 the government set up the London Docklands Development Corporation (LDDC) to tackle urban renewal in the east of London. Thus the Green Belt, somewhat accidently, became part of the broader urban policy objectives – a key point that was to be developed further in the Urban Task Force Report in 1999.[45]

By the 1990s Green Belts were beginning to present problems in relation to the population growth of major cities, most notably London. Policy makers therefore deemed it necessary to update the definition of Green Belt and to redefine how best it should function. Planning Policy Guidance Note 2 (PPG 2, 1995), an update of Circular 14/84 (consolidated in PPG 2, 1988), referred to the earlier Circular 42/55 as 'historic', but completely omitted any reference to land purchase or greater public access to the countryside. The five purposes of Green Belt were defined as:

- Checking unrestricted sprawl
- Preventing neighbouring towns from merging
- Safeguarding the countryside from encroachment
- Preserving the setting of historic towns
- Assisting in the recycling of derelict urban land

This was a far more limited definition of the Green Belt than the aspirations of the 1920s and 1930s. The primary vehicle for controlling Green Belt was through designation in local plans. There were no pro-active government programmes to facilitate opening up public access and, in a period of constraint on public expenditure, local authorities were certainly not awash with funds. At this point the original purposes of the Green Belt – a progressive policy to open up public access to the countryside for urban populations – had become a regressive policy to restrict the growth of cities and preserve the amenity of the more prosperous communities living on the urban periphery and in the countryside. No wonder that it was popular with a particular segment of the electorate.

A revised Planning Policy Guidance – PPG 2[46]– did, however, reflect a more complex agenda than that of the 1980s. The environmental movement had received considerable impetus by the Rio Summit[47] and the importance of the countryside for biodiversity was included in the objectives of the Green Belt:

a) to provide opportunities for access to the open countryside for the urban population
b) to provide opportunities for outdoor sport and outdoor recreation near urban areas
c) to retain attractive landscapes, and enhance landscapes, near to where people live

d) to improve damaged and derelict land around towns
e) to secure nature conservation interest
f) to retain land in agricultural, forestry and related uses

In 2012 PPG 2 was superseded by the National Planning Policy Framework (NPPF).[48] Broadly the objectives of the Green Belt remained the same as in PPG 2, with development being acceptable only in 'very special circumstances'. The NPPF did allow appropriate buildings for agriculture and recreation, as well as minor extensions to existing buildings and accepted limited infilling in villages, plus limited affordable housing for local community needs. This reflected new concerns around the Green Belt, particularly the desire by government to allow more house building on greenfield sites. The implications of this are considered further in chapter 3.

The Green Belt has been successful in relation to urban containment in the post-war period, but in the process has reduced the supply of developable land. This has redirected development to brownfield sites that might otherwise have remained derelict. Circular 14/84 had advocated higher density developments within the city as part of a strategy to regenerate depressed areas and bring social and economic benefits. Economic benefits include: [49]

- Minimised costs for the provision of road and services (electrical, water, etc.) infrastructure
- Increasing the viability of transportation systems and related infrastructure

The Urban Task Force under Richard Rogers developed these ideas further.[50] The Task Force looked towards the European model of the compact city rather than a model of dispersed development. The report advocated the importance of public (especially civic) space, walking, cycling and public transport, as well as mixed use development. It endorsed restrictions on the outward sprawl of cities and the reuse of brownfield land. The rationale did not arise from a fear of urban growth, nor from a misplaced nostalgia for a rural idyll. The fundamental vision of the Task Force was the *renaissance* of the city – a renaissance that would be jeopardised by outward growth that left inner areas derelict and poor. Reusing infrastructure within the city was seen as an absolute necessity, as was environmental sustainability. A compact city could intensify its use of infrastructure, minimise car use *and* preserve open space, both within the city and beyond, for agriculture, recreation and ecology.

In 2000 Richard Rogers was appointed as the adviser on architecture and urbanism by Ken Livingstone, the first Mayor of London under the reconstituted GLA. Thus the ideas of the Urban Task Force were fed directly into the first London Plan, 2004.

The London Plan (revised and amended in 2008, 2011 and 2016) still endorses the concept of a Green Belt.[51] The Mayor 'strongly supports the current extent of the London green belt, its extension in appropriate circumstances and its protection from inappropriate development'. Over the life of the GLA this policy approach has remained consistent,[52] but it has been integrated into a broader and more complex policy framework around green infrastructure (Fig. 1.7). The East London Green Grid[53] was produced in 2006 by Design for London as a concept to improve and upgrade urban open spaces for nature conservation and recreation and connect them together. It has since been extended

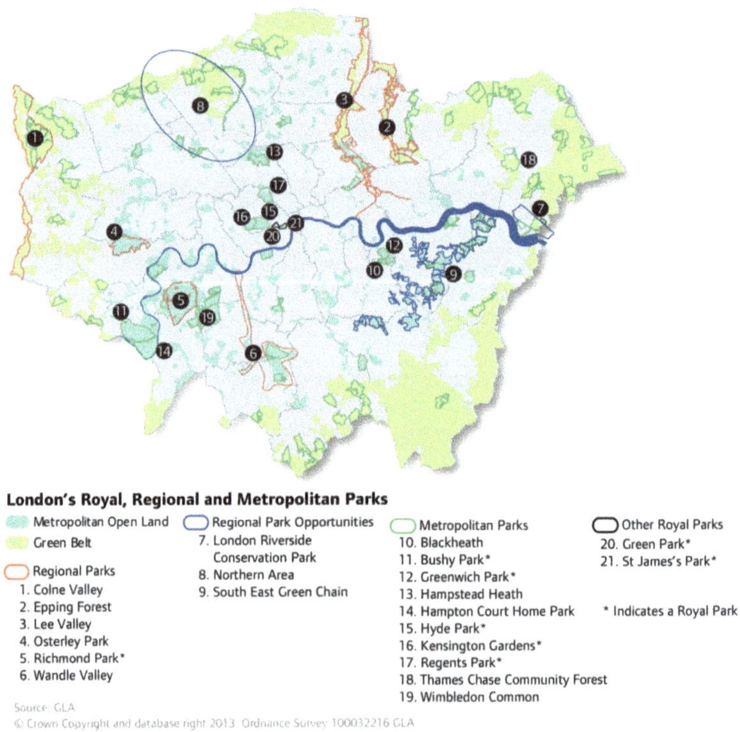

Fig. 1.7 Map of London's Strategic Open Space Network. *Source: The London Plan*, 2016 (GLA).

to cover all of London. London Plan policies recognise the importance of biodiversity, natural drainage, rivers, culture, food production and historic landscapes. Critically the Plan now links of all of these to strategies to address climate change and promote health and wellbeing.

Green Belt – a neutral or political policy?

It is tempting to try to interpret Green Belt policy in party political terms. The concept of a Green Belt for London, focused as it then was on public access, came from the LCC under the Labour politician Herbert Morrison. He was later to serve in the Attlee government (1945–51) and oversaw much of the nationalisation programme. However, a look at the voting characteristics of urban areas, as opposed to the suburbs and the near-urban countryside, shows a clear political and social class divide. It might be an exaggeration to describe Conservative politicians as being anti-urban, but they do reflect the perspectives of their constituencies who often view the city with suspicion – a place to be contained in case it devours their Arcadian idyll or, worse, swamps them with a dangerous and undesirable urban underclass. The attitudes of Howard are still evident in these political groupings, which perceive the countryside as both the ideal abode and a place to be enjoyed by a privileged few.

By 1995 there were 1,556,000 acres of Green Belt in England, covering almost 12 per cent of the country. While comparison of designated Green Belt with the political control of parliamentary constituencies (Figs 1.8 and 1.9) is inevitably a crude comparison, there is a correlation. This is reflected in the attitudes of the Conservative Party in upholding the integrity of the Green Belt, despite lobbying from the housebuilding industry.

The Conservative government between 1979 and 1997 reflected the perspective of the countryside in many of its policies. The abolition of the GLC in 1986 deprived London of metropolitan administration. Infrastructure projects such as the M25 linked peripheral settlements around London and there was a general policy shift in favour of the private car. The growth of out-of-town shopping looked more to the North American model of land use planning than the European. However, there were exceptions. The inner-city riots in Brixton and Toxteth in 1981 made a stark impression on Michael Heseltine (Secretary of State for the Environment, 1979–83), who recognised that the decline of inner urban areas could not be ignored. Heseltine appreciated that a policy of managed decline of inner-city areas was not a sustainable option and set up Enterprise

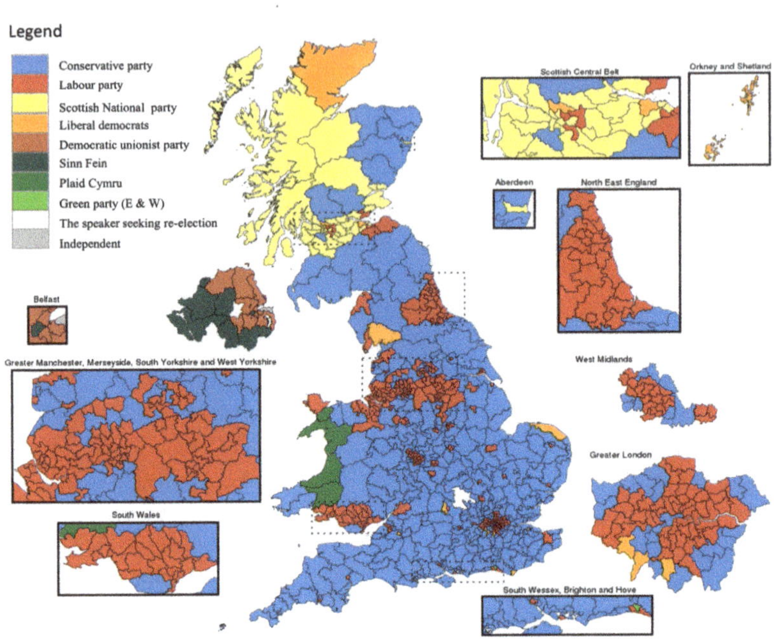

Fig. 1.8 Map showing political control of Parliamentary constituencies after the 2017 General Election. CC BY-SA 4.0.

Areas and Development Corporations in Merseyside and East London. The addition to Circular 14/84 of a new function for Green Belts in 'assisting in the recycling of derelict urban land' reflects this shift in policy.

The election of the Labour Party to power in 1997 signalled a clear shift of emphasis back towards addressing the needs of the city. The Urban Task Force's radical rethink of urban policy was part of the agenda of the newly elected Labour government. The new policy emphasis is summed up in 1999 by John Prescott, the Deputy Prime Minister, in his preface to the report:

> Over the past few decades many of our urban areas have suffered neglect and decline with an exodus from the inner cities, driven by a lack of confidence in schools, fear of crime, an unhealthy environment and poor housing. This is bad for our people, bad for quality of life, bad for our economy and bad for our society.[54]

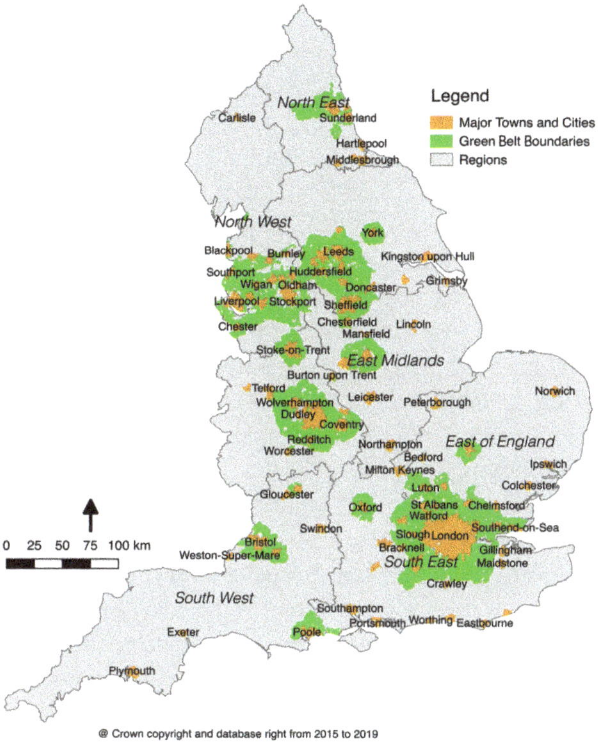

Fig. 1.9 Map showing Green Belt and major urban areas in England from a report by Natural England and the Campaign to Protect Rural England, 2010.

Source: Natural England. *Green Belts: A greener future. A report by Natural England and the Campaign to Protect Rural England (CPRE)*, 2010, p.15.

The Labour government did not propose scrapping Green Belts, but did review the policy in the Town and Country Planning (Green Belt) Direction, 2005. While endorsing the general principle, and certainly not reverting back to the earlier policy of land purchase for recreation and amenity, it did propose a relaxation of policies concerning development on the Green Belt, stating that a local authority should decide whether 'the development would *significantly* impact on the openness of the green belt'. It proposed that small-scale developments of under 1,000 square metres might be acceptable in certain locations.

The Green Belt today

The 2018 updates to the National Planning Policy Framework (NPPF) offer practical guidance with regards to development in the Green Belt. The mandate for Green Belts has remained largely unchanged, however, since the introduction of the NPPF in 2012. More recent updates to the NPPF in 2019 largely concern oil, gas and coal exploration and extraction. Key issues have been sidestepped, most notably those concerning the escalating housing crisis – the limited supply of affordable new homes. Yet shifts in emphasis starting to take place within government demonstrate concern over the constraints that Green Belt designation places on development, house building in particular. The growing housing supply crisis in the UK is placing new demands for the release of land for development.

While in theory there is still sufficient brownfield land to accommodate the requirements for new housing, there is also a growing lobby, particularly from the volume house builders, for the release of greenfield sites. Such sites are perceived to be cheaper and less risky to develop, and there is certainly a demand for the lower density family housing that could be accommodated on them. The Conservative government is being lobbied from its electoral heartlands to resist development and from the housebuilders (many of whom were major donors to party funds) to allow it. This conundrum is explored further in chapter 3.

The impact of present Green Belt policy is being felt in London. The rapid population growth (from less than 7 million in 1983 to 9.18 million in 2019)[55] is resulting in a shortage of land for housing. The first London Plan of 2004 identified opportunity areas that correlated roughly to the largest brownfield sites and were reflected in the housing quotas set for the boroughs. But the policy of not encroaching on the Green Belt has pushed up average new development densities to levels not seen before in the capital. Table 1.2 shows the steady increase in residential densities under successive London Plans, and a large increase in high-rise developments. In 2014 the London Skyline Campaign launched to 'stop the devastation of London' counted 242 high-rise buildings (over 20 storeys) within London. The Campaign raised concerns on their impact on the historic character of the area and the Thames.

The relationship between the increase in residential densities in London, the construction of tall buildings and the preservation of the Green Belt (regardless of the intrinsic quality of parts of it) should be clear. If London cannot expand outwards it will become denser and, since density

Table 1.2 Increase in London residential densities (1966–2011)

London 1996/99	00/03	04/08	08/09	09/11
Average residential density dwellings per ha	over previous	over previous	over previous	over previous
57	+ 36%	+34%	+33%	+144%

Source: Gordon et al. 'Defining, Measuring and Implementing Density Standards in London', London Plan Density Research Project 1, 2016.

caps have largely been discarded by the London Plan, buildings will become taller. The policy of restricting the outward growth of London in order to concentrate development activity into brownfield land is, of course, still valid. However, it is now almost 40 years since it was introduced and as brownfield land is developed urban densities will continue to rise.

Many factors – income levels, demographics and design – allow high-density developments to work effectively, but there do have to be limits and some areas of London, often the poorer areas, are approaching them. Two further changes are also impacting on the ability of London to contain its growth within its urban boundaries. The first is the dismantling of the government agencies charged with regional development. Limiting urban growth might help to concentrate investment back into inner urban areas, but a lot of brownfield land suffered from levels of contamination and poor access that mitigated against its development. The Regional Development Agencies (and before this English Partnerships) were able to intervene to remediate land for development, but these were abolished by the Conservative government in 2011. Second, affordable housing was grant-subsidised by the Homes and Communities Agency. From the late 1990s the level of subsidy was reduced by the Labour government; it has now been removed completely. In the absence of any assistance to improve the provision of affordable housing on tough, inner-city brownfield sites, the solution has been to pile on the density. HTA architects advise against schemes at densities greater than 350 homes per hectare,[56] which they categorise as 'hyperdensity'. However, the London Plan (2016) suggests that densities of 650–1100 hrh in central London might be acceptable – well over three times the HTA recommendation.

There is now a squeeze in London to accommodate excessive densities on sites that are difficult and costly to develop. Amid the housing crisis, calls for 'relaxing' Green Belt policy are growing. A trickle of proposals for new homes on London's Green Belt have been submitted and in many cases approved. Planning applications for the construction of 35,000 additional homes on the UK's Green Belts were submitted in 2018. Over 24,000 new homes have been constructed on Green Belt land over the past nine years; construction on Green Belt land effectively doubled in 2017. As Urbanist Architecture reported in 2019, 'getting planning permission to build on the Green Belt may be tricky [*sic*] but it's certainly not impossible'.[57]

Conclusions

This chapter has provided an overview of the evolution of the Green Belt as a planning concept and the implications of the policy for London. In many ways the Green Belt is one of the great achievements of post-war planning. It has prevented urban sprawl and ribbon development and is undoubtedly popular with the public. There is a general concern about the loss of countryside to development, particularly as environmental sustainability rises up the public agenda.

Wikipedia sums up the popular definition of the purpose of Green Belt:

> In British town planning, the green belt is a policy for controlling urban growth. The idea is for a ring of countryside where urbanisation will be resisted for the foreseeable future, maintaining an area where agriculture, forestry and outdoor leisure can be expected to prevail.

This demonstrates a significant move away from the original purpose of Green Belt. It is also an extremely narrow definition to limit the function of Green Belt to urban containment. It ignores the far wider agenda of the relationship of the city to its hinterland in terms of ecology, resource management and resilience. Indeed, the whole environmental debate concerning the value and use of 'countryside', and the relative prioritisation of the social needs of rural against urban populations, is conveniently ignored in such a narrow definition.

The Green Belt is both a response to unregulated urban expansion and a resource to compensate for the perceived disadvantages of urban living. These two functions came to the fore at the turn of the 20th century with Ebenezer Howard's Garden City. His idealised new settlements were divided by green land, not only to create a physical boundary to regulate the urban population, but also to provide space for agriculture.

Many of Howard's concepts have been carried over into the UK planning system and remain remarkably constant to the present day. The unchanged nature of both policy *and attitudes* to Green Belts raise serious questions about their function in the light of London's housing crisis. Indeed, some academics and industry experts suggest that they are a major contributor to the housing crisis.

The arguments for Green Belt to control urban sprawl are clear, and this has been a major success of the policy. Sprawl and ribbon development have been largely avoided and individual settlements around the periphery of London have retained their character and identity. The control of urban sprawl by Green Belts has generated higher development densities through the promotion of infill developments; it has also assisted in the recycling of brownfield land and the optimisation of existing transport infrastructure and utilities. Theoretically, shorter commuting times are not only more sustainable but also increase social cohesion. Very significant costs have been avoided through the use of existing roads and rail infrastructure. Congestion, one of the concerns of the Abercrombie Plan, has been partly mitigated.

There are clear environmental benefits in retaining Green Belts, particularly the proximity of agriculture to the urban population, water management, mitigation of the urban heat island effect and biodiversity. The preservation of open countryside does not guarantee public access or biodiversity, and there are large areas of Green Belt that are deficient in both of these. The use of agricultural land, for food production or nature conservation, is becoming important in light of sustainable food production in post-Brexit Britain.

The future of Green Belts from a policy perspective is far from secure. The political mood is swinging against the enlightened ideals that saw the creation of the Green Belt, with the countryside being viewed by some as a 'yet to be developed' void around the city and as a 'commodity' that could be developed for housing. Over the last 25 years successive governments have weakened the legislation that underpins the Green Belt. Has this great experiment in enlightened planning policy outlived its usefulness? Or are there new purposes for open land around our cities?

Alternative models for Green Belt policy have been developed around the world resulting from very different planning approaches, urban forms and mechanisms; these are explored in chapter 2. Chapter 3 considers how the Green Belt is becoming a political battleground and ways in which policy might develop in response. Climate change is raising serious issues concerning the resilience of cities to both extreme weather events and the impact of rising global temperatures. The relationship of the city with its hinterland is likely to change as radically in the next 50 years as when city walls were dismantled at the end of the 18th century. The changing relationship of cities with their hinterlands is explored in chapter 4.

It is clear that the relationship of the city to its regional hinterland has become a lot more complicated since the 19th century.

Notes

1. Horace, *Odes* III, 29.11.
2. Krieger 1953, 300–14.
3. Rasmussen 1982.
4. Chadwick 1842.
5. Engels 1850.
6. Briggs 1963, 75.
7. Dickens 1854.
8. Booth 1889.
9. Alison 1825.
10. The Octavia Hill Society archive, 2020.
11. Hill 1883.
12. The National Trust 2017/18.
13. Epping Forest Act 1878.
14. On 6 May 1882 (News Shopper 2002).
15. McInnes 2011.
16. Howard 1902.
17. Howard 1902.
18. Frey 2000.
19. Larkfleet Group 2015.
20. Thomas 1963.
21. This led to subsequent legislation to establish National Parks (1949) and the Countryside and Right to Roam Act (2000).
22. IFHTP 1935; Pepler 1935; Riboldazzi, 2010; cited in Geertse, 2015.
23. Geertse 2015.
24. Amati and Makoto 2007.
25. Amati and Makoto 2007.
26. Bailey and Baxter 2016.
27. LCC archives.
28. Today's Community Infrastructure Levy or Section 106 agreements.
29. Amati and Makoto 2007.
30. Abercrombie 1944.
31. Abercrombie 1944.
32. Abercrombie 1944.
33. Campaign from the Ministry of Food in 1941 to encourage individuals to grow their own food in response to wartime food shortages.
34. MHLG 1955.
35. MHLG 1955.

36. Edwards 2016.
37. Hall 2002.
38. Echenique et al. 2012.
39. Department for Transport 2019.
40. London County Council 1960.
41. Greater London Council 1969.
42. For example, Mile End Park in Tower Hamlets, Burgess Park in Southwark and Barnard Park in Islington.
43. MHLG 1955.
44. Department of the Environment 1984.
45. Urban Task Force 1999.
46. ODPM 2001.
47. UNCED 1992.
48. MHCLG, 2012.
49. Rydin and Myerson 1989.
50. Urban Task Force 1999.
51. GLA 2016.
52. Despite the tenure of three different Mayors: Ken Livingstone (Labour) 2000–8; Boris Johnson (Conservative) 2008–16; Sadiq Khan (Labour) 2016–present.
53. GLA 2006.
54. Urban Task Force 1999, Preface.
55. UN Department of Economic and Social Affairs 2019.
56. HTA 2015.
57. Urbanist Architecture 2019.

References

Abercrombie, Patrick. *Greater London Plan, 1944*. London: University of London Press, 1944.

Alison, Archibald. *Essays on the Nature and Principles of Taste*, 6th ed. Printed by the heirs of D. Willison for A. Constable; London: Longman, Hurst, Rees, Orme, Brown & Green, 1825.

Amati, M. and Makoto, Y. 'The Establishment of the London Green Belt', *Journal of Planning History* 6 (4) (2007): 311–37.

Bailey, I. and Baxter, J. *90 Years of Farmland Values and Supply*. 26 April 2016. https://www.savills.co.uk/research_articles/229130/202022-0. Last modified 12 February 2020.

Booth, Charles. *Life and Labour of the People*. Vol. I, 1889; Vol. 2, 1891. London: Macmillan, 1902–3 (complete volumes).

Briggs, Asa. *Victorian Cities*. London: Odhams Press Limited, 1963, 75. Reprinted by Penguin Books, 1968.

Chadwick, Edwin. *A Report on the Sanitary Conditions of the Labouring Population*. 1842.

Department of the Environment. *Green Belts*, Circular 14/84. London: HMSO, 1984.

Department of Transport. *GB Road Traffic Counts*, May 2019. https://www.gov.uk/government/collections/road-traffic-statistics. Last modified 12 February 2020.

Dickens, Charles. *Hard Times*. 1854.

Echenique, M.H., Hargreaves, A.J., Mitchell, G. and Namdeo, A. 'Growing Cities Sustainably: Does urban form really matter?', *Journal of the American Planning Association* 78 (2) (2012): 121–37.

Edwards, M. 'The Housing Crisis and London', *City* 20 (2) (2016): 222–37.

Engels, Friedrich. *The Condition of the Working Class in England in 1844*. Harmondsworth: Penguin Classics, 1987 [1850].

Epping Forest Act 1878. https://www.cityoflondon.gov.uk/things-to-do/green-spaces/epping-forest/about-us/Documents/1878-Epping-Forest-Act.pdf. Accessed 12 February 2020.

Frey, H.W. 'Not Green Belts but Green Wedges: The precarious relationship between city and country', *Urban Design International* 5 (1) (2000): 13–25.

Geertse M. 'Cross Border Planning Dialogue in Interwar Europe', *SAGE*. Open July–September 2015: 1–12. https://journals.sagepub.com/doi/pdf/10.1177/2158244015600768. Accessed 12 February 2020.

Gordon, I., Mace, A. and Whitehead, C. 'Defining, Measuring and Implementing Density Standards in London'. London Plan Density Research Project 1, LSE, London, July 2016. http://www.lse.ac.uk/business-and-consultancy/consulting/assets/documents/london-plan-density-research-project-1.pdf. Accessed 12 February 2020.
Greater London Authority (GLA). *East London Green Grid Primer*, November 2006.
Greater London Authority (GLA). *London Plan*, 2016. https://www.london.gov.uk/sites/default/files/map_2.8_open_space_network.pdf
Greater London Council (GLC). *Tomorrow's London. A background to the Greater London Development Plan*. County Hall, London, 1969.
Hall, P. *Cities of Tomorrow: An intellectual history of urban planning and design in the twentieth century*. Oxford: Blackwell Publishing, 2002.
Hill, Octavia. 'Space for the People'. In *Homes of the London Poor*, edited by Octavia Hill. London: Macmillan and Co., 1883 [1875].
Horace, *Odes III* 29.11.
Howard, Ebenezer. *To-Morrow: A peaceful path to real reform*. London: S. Sonnenschein & Co. Ltd., 1898.
Howard, Ebenezer. *Garden Cities of Tomorrow*. London: S. Sonnenschein & Co. Ltd., 1902.
HTA. *Super Density: The sequel*. London: HTA, 2015. https://www.pollardthomasedwards.co.uk/download/SUPERDENSITY_2015_download.pdf. Accessed 12 February 2020.
International Federation for Housing and Town Planning. XIV International Housing and Town Planning Congress, London, 1935.
Krieger, Murray. 'The Ambiguous Anti-Romanticism of T.E. Hulme', *ELH* 20 (4) (1953): 300–14.
Larkfleet Group. *Building Sustainability*, August 2015. https://larkfleet.com/larkfleetgroup/building-sustainability/. Accessed 12 February 2020.
London County Council. *Administrative County of London Development Plan First Review 1960*. London: London County Council, 1960.
McInnes, I. 'On the Street Where You Live', *The Dulwich Society Journal*, 2011. https://www.dulwichsociety.com/journal-archive/71-spring-2011/608-ildersly-grove. Accessed 12 February 2020.
Ministry of Housing and Local Government (MHLG). *Green Belts*, Circular 42/55. London: HMSO, 1955.
Ministry of Housing, Communities and Local Government (MHCLG). *National Planning Policy Framework*, 27 March 2012 (revised 19 June 2019). https://www.gov.uk/government/publications/national-planning-policy-framework--2. Accessed 20 January 2020.
The National Trust, *Annual Report 2017/18*. https://nt.global.ssl.fastly.net/documents/annual-report-201718.pdf. Accessed 12 February 2020.
Natural England. *Green Belts: A greener future. A report by Natural England and the Campaign to Protect Rural England (CPRE)*. 2010, 15. http://publications.naturalengland.org.uk/search?q=green+belt&num=100.
News Shopper. *Queen Victoria's Visit to Epping Forest*. 5 April 2002. https://www.newsshopper.co.uk/news/6345576.queen-victorias-visit-to-epping-forest/. Accessed 12 February 2020.
Octavia Hill Society Archive. *Conservation*. http://www.octaviahill.org/about-octavia-hill/conservation/. Accessed 12 February 2020.
Office of the Deputy Prime Minister (ODPM), Planning Policy Guidance 2 (PPG 2). *Green Belts*. January 1995 (amended March 2001). https://webarchive.nationalarchives.gov.uk/20120920011651/; http://www.communities.gov.uk/documents/planningandbuilding/pdf/155499.pdf.
Pepler, G. L. 'International Federation for Housing and Town Planning', *Journal of the Town Planning Institute* 21 (1935): 275–8.
Rasmussen, Steen Eiler. *London the Unique City*. Cambridge, MA: The MIT Press, 1982.
Riboldazzi, R. *Un'altra modernità: L'IFHTP e la cultura urbanistica tra le due guerre 1923–1939* [*Another modernity: the IFHTP and the town planning culture between the wars*]. Rome: Gangemi, 2010: 138–40.
Rydin, Y. and Myerson, G. 'Explaining and Interpreting Ideological Effects: A rhetorical approach to green belts', *Environment and Planning D: Society and Space* 7 (4) (1989): 463–79.
Thomas, D. 'London's Green Belt: The evolution of an idea', *The Geographical Journal* 129 (1) (1963): 14–24.

United Nations Conference on Environment and Development (UNCED) Rio Earth Summit, June 1992. Report of the United Nations Conference of Environment and Development: Vol.1. Resolutions of Conference. New York: United Nations, 1993.

United Nations Department of Economic and Social Affairs. *World Urbanisation Prospects*. New York: United Nations, 2019. https://population.un.org/wpp/Publications/Files/WPP2019_Highlights.pdf. Accessed 12 February 2020.

Urban Task Force. *Towards an Urban Renaissance*. London: HMSO, 1999.

Urbanist Architecture. *Green Belt Planning Permission in the UK*, 2019. https://urbanistarchitecture.co.uk/how-to-get-planning-permission-for-building-on-greenbelt-land-in-the-uk/. Accessed 12 February 2020.

'Vienna 1858'. *A Handbook for Travellers in Southern Germany*, 8th ed. London: John Murray, 1858. http://www.1uptravel.com/worldmaps/history-europe71.html.

Wikimedia Commons. https://commons.wikimedia.org/wiki/File:2017UKElectionMap.svg.

Chapter 2
Garden Cities, suburbs and fringes: the Green Belt in a global setting

Alona Martinez Perez

Today 60% of the European urban population live outside the limits of the city that was built and consolidated by the end of the second half of the last century.

Boeri 2011, 29–30

Introduction

The Green Belt in London comprises a vast area. It incorporates London's suburban fringe and extends into the city region covering parts of eight counties. This large area of protected land was created originally to restrict urban growth from London and to safeguard the countryside from development. Concentric in nature, the Green Belt has grown significantly since its creation.

There are two views in the English psyche about the Green Belt: one is a romanticised view of protecting a beautiful, 'natural' landscape and the other is a pragmatic approach to limit the growth and extent of the city. These views go back to the origins of thinking on modern town and country planning at the beginning of the 20th century. The town was where people lived and worked – a busy, intensely social place with a mix of uses, social and cultural activities and high- and low-density housing. The countryside, by contrast, was a place for nature, agriculture and recreation, a place in which to relax and enjoy oneself. This is a utopian and nostalgic view of the Green Belt. In reality the vast area of Green Belt around London is a mix of both farmland and brownfield areas, as well as left over industrial space. It is far from the idealised view of English countryside that has dominated Green Belt thinking for the last 80 years. The designation of the Green Belt around London and other English cities was largely a restrictive measure. It has stopped any rational debate around proactive scenarios or development of this land, whether for housing or any other purpose.

The rationale that underpins the Green Belt in the UK cannot easily be separated from Ebenezer Howard's ideas of the 'Garden City'. This was an idealised place with beautiful (family) housing, tree-lined streets and healthy and productive lifestyles. In many ways this is also the suburban typology that resulted from the rapid growth of London in the early 20th century. The suburb may have had similarities with Howard's Garden City, but often the reality was an urban sprawl of bland suburban streets and low-density housing more closely aligned with the generic American model of car-reliant suburbia. The Green Belt was brought into existence in part to prevent this model from extending ever further over the countryside that surrounded cities.

This chapter will compare different approaches to Green Belts in the city region and contrast different interpretations of the idea between the UK, other European countries, Asia and North America. It will consider different approaches to containment and urban sprawl, the resultant urban edge condition and urban spatial form. It will trace the interchange of ideas between European and English models of urban theory and compare the alternative models of spatial thinking of Richard Rogers and Peter Hall with Manuel de Solà-Morales. By way of illustration it will refer to two extensive case studies of Madrid and Johannesburg. The chapter concludes by comparing the strengths of alternative spatial forms for the urban edge and region.

The Green Belt in urban planning

The function of the Green Belt can be described as follows:

> Green belts were originally seen in controlling further urban growth, in avoiding the merge of cities into each other and in separating the typical characters of town and countryside.[1]

At the beginning of the 20th century, when Green Belts were first proposed, the differentiation between town and country was clearer in English cities than today. The centre was a place for work and the periphery a place for living. At the heart of this urban typology is the perceived desirability of the single family house in the suburb with its front and back garden. This concept is engrained in English culture. Peter Hall (Bartlett Professor of Planning and Regeneration, UCL and eminent British urbanist) writes in relation to Howard:

> The advantages of the city were the opportunities it offered in the form of accessibility to jobs and to urban services of all kinds; the disadvantages could all be summed up in the poor resulting natural environment. Conversely, the countryside offered an excellent environment but virtually no opportunities of any sort.[2]

The resilience of the Garden City as an ideal is surprising when considered against the changes that have taken place in the economic and social structure of the city over the past hundred years. Similarly, the purpose and function of Green Belt has also changed since then. It was introduced as a reserve of open land for the enjoyment of urban populations, but has evolved to become an instrument to prevent the growth of the city (regardless of the consequences for those living in it). In order to chart these changes and assess possible future scenarios for the Green Belt it is worth looking at the spatial characteristics of Green Belts with specific reference to urban edges and suburbs.

The Green Belt is both a zone and an edge: it can surround the city and separate urban corridors. By looking at the definitions of edge, strip and corridor we can understand the urban conditions that appear spatially within the Green Belt. Kevin Lynch defines the edges of a city in his seminal work *The Image of the City*: 'Edges are the linear elements not considered as paths: they are usually the boundaries between two kinds of areas. They act as lateral references'.[3] As an example of an edge in a city he refers to the Charles River in Boston, describing it as 'the best example' which 'has all of those qualities'. The edge in Boston is delimited by the river, a physical and geographical presence in the city.

This probably has a greater presence in the morphology of the city than Boston's 'Emerald Necklace' – its Green Belt. Lynch then considers Chicago, a city that also has a Green Belt, observing that 'It would be interesting to see how many Chicagoans would begin to draw a map of their city by putting down something other than the line of the lake shore'. For most Londoners the Green Belt as an edge is not clearly defined in their minds. It is not a presence in the city that can be recognised as an urban edge, nor is it a place where people gather or meet up. Instead it is an arbitrary line defined on a map that marks a *legislative* edge of the city where planning controls stop further urban growth.

The Spanish architect Manuel de Solà-Morales i Rubió, a former Professor at the ETSAB (Barcelona School of Architecture), was one of the most important urban planners of his generation. He had a particular interest in the outskirts and peripheries of cities. Among many contributions to urban thinking he coined the term *terrain vague* to describe the condition of the peri-urban fringe that was neither city nor countryside. His ideas on the urban fringe were set out in *Las formas de crecimiento urbano* (*Forms of urban growth*), a classic text in Spain today.[4] The book (never translated into English) offers a clear understanding of urban and economic processes and interventions associated with urban growth. Solà-Morales' work poses critical questions concerning the principles of the Garden City. He argues that the Garden City is not a final solution, but rather an intermediate position between city and country. It does not unlock the potential of the city, but instead moves the housing issue into the country. The spatial layout of the Garden City is a series of concentric rings around the existing central core surrounded by an industrial ring and then a green one. These are defined and held in place by planning principles that control both the use of land and ownership. These principles of control and concentric development are analogous to those that protect the Green Belt.

The approach to simple zoning that underlies Howard's thinking has now become largely outmoded. In the second half of the 20th century the focus has shifted away from the imposed utopian condition of the Garden City. Instead it deals with the problems of the city through regeneration programmes that seek solutions *within* the urban fabric. As Hebbert writes:

> The counterplan for Poble Nou published by Manuel de Solà-Morales and colleagues in 1974 was one of Europe's earliest systematic exercises in repair of an urban quarter. Solà-Morales recalls the radical impact within Barcelona next year, when Philippe Panerai and Jean Castex published the first edition of *Formes Urbains*, their powerful study of the 'agony' of the European street block. Over the next three decades Barcelona's Laboratorio de Urbanismo would be an international centre of excellence, both for its practical assistance to towns and neighbourhoods wrestling with development pressure and as the Iberian point of entry for practitioners such as Aldo Rossi, Carlo Aynomino (IUAV, Venice), Philippe Panerai (Versailles) and Josef-Paul Kleihues (IBA-Berlin).[5]

The experience of Barcelona was to have a profound impact on the thinking of Richard Rogers (discussed below). While there may still be a clear rationale for protecting the Green Belt, the city today is much more complex. The many layers and complexities of a modern city such as London cannot be understood from the simplicity of a diagram that is over a century old. The idea of concentric zones around the city centre might have made sense in the past, but no longer meets the needs of the modern metropolis. The industrial zones of European cities in the early 20th century have now largely disappeared; industry is no longer a major polluter there and mixed use, fine-grained urban typologies have become the predominant urban form for the 21st century. We can no longer base development on historical examples. While they are interesting as past experiments, they do not make sense in today's post-industrial economy.

Chapter 1 has traced the history of the development of the Green Belt in the UK from the end of the 19th century to the present day. It is not strictly true, however, to claim that the idea was invented in England. The contrast between town and countryside dates back to the beginning of cities and was particularly clear where city defences were required, whether in ancient Mesopotamia, Rome, medieval Europe or China. Even where a city had defensive walls, informal uses and settlements often formed a peripheral zone around the city – but these have long since disappeared. The limitations of transport made the proximity of open agricultural land important. In some cases royal estates or hunting grounds, such as the Vienna Woods, Hyde Park and the Bois de Boulogne, existed beyond the city limits and have now become parks within the city or on its periphery.

This chapter does not seek to provide an exhaustive analysis of Green Belts around the world, but rather to outline alternative approaches to Green Belts that have developed in different countries. These have all grown out of common concerns about urban growth that originated in the early 20th century and are still taking place today. There are four broad categories of Green Belts which are explored further below:

- The urban parkland (Mumbai, Stockholm and Adelaide). These are largely recreational and are not designed to universally restrict sprawl
- The urban limit (Korea and China). These are planning measures to restrict sprawl, but are largely non-prescriptive about the nature and function of the land beyond the urban edge
- The Green Belt (Oregon, Ottawa, London and the Randstad). These are integrated planning responses that both limit urban sprawl and

protect the countryside for recreational, amenity and agricultural purposes
- The environmental barrier (Germany and China). These are regional landscape initiatives that are not connected to metropolitan areas

Proto-Green Belts: parklands, agriculture and National Parks

One of the earliest examples of a proto-Green Belt was William Light's 1837 plan for Adelaide. This established formal city squares and gardens within the city and parklands in the surrounding landscape. The plan for Adelaide created a ring of over 1,000 acres of parklands around the city: Adelaide Park. This was placed in the hands of the municipal authorities in 1852. It is no accident that other Commonwealth countries such as New Zealand and India adopted the concept of parklands at the edge of the city. Early examples in the former include Wellington (1840), Dunedin (1848) and Hamilton (1877); these remain important open spaces that shape these cities today. They are not Green Belts in the present sense of the term, but rather an integrated part of the enlightened planning of new settlements, often on 'virgin land'. Many Indian cities, including Delhi, Mumbai and Chennai, have large, safeguarded national parks that serve as 'green lungs' for the cities.[6] However, these are more akin to National Parks than formal Green Belts. In the Americas cities such as Sao Paolo and Santo Dominigo also have such Green Belts, which again take the form of protected National Forests.

In Europe the idea of the urban park and civic square (often restricted to wealthy users) stretches back a long way. The dismantling of city fortifications towards the end of the 19th century allowed some circular city parks to be established, such as the Ringstrasse in Vienna and the Inner and Outer 'Green Girdles' (*Grungurtel*) in Cologne. This was also a period in which enlightened city planning provided metropolitan parks within the new neighbourhoods of the city. Unlike earlier urban parks these were to be open to the public.

The idea that urban populations should have access to the fresh air and leisure opportunities of the countryside also gained traction at this time. Chapter 1 covers this in more detail, in particular European thinking on the relationship between the city and the countryside expressed in the International Federation of Housing and Town Planning conferences. This led to early attempts to create open spaces on the edges of cities. In Frankfurt, for example, an early Green Belt was established in the 1920s under the direction of Ernst May as part of a comprehensive landscape plan along the city's two rivers.

The first example of a Green Belt in America was in Boston. Here, in 1878, a 440-hectare network of public parks known as the 'Emerald Necklace' was created. In 1909 a huge public park system was proposed for Chicago that extended beyond the city into the surrounding region. These early examples of landscape strategies associated with city planning are, like the proto-Green Belts in Australia and New Zealand, parklands close to the city, designed for the recreation and enjoyment of urban populations. In the recession of the 1930s Roosevelt's New Deal created a series of Garden City settlements. Greenbelt, Maryland was established in 1935, to be followed soon afterwards by Greendale, Wisconsin and Greenhills, Ohio. They were based on Howard's ideals of communities that combined housing, work and leisure.

Each of these new towns was surrounded by a belt of open, largely agricultural land. In post-war America a Green Belt more analogous to the English model was created in Lexington, Kentucky (1958). Its purpose was to safeguard farmland used for horse breeding from urban encroachment.[7] Green Belts are now a relatively common feature in American cities. The states of Oregon, Washington and Tennessee all require cities to establish 'urban growth boundaries' to restrict sprawl and protect farmland and forests.

A number of European cities have designated parklands or protected open land on their periphery. Examples include the *Parco Agricola Sud Milano,* an arc of 47 square kilometres of protected land to the south of Milan. The Royal National City Park to the north of Stockholm similarly provides an edge to the north and protects forest and countryside for the enjoyment of urban populations. The Emescher Park in the Ruhr was created between 1989–99 by Peter Latz. This is a regenerated landscape that forms part of a regional forest around the old mining and steel cities of Essen, Bochum and Duisburg. Its main purpose, however, is for recreation and environmental enhancement, not the prevention of urban sprawl; these cities are not expanding and have a surplus of brownfield sites. None of these examples are Green Belts in the English sense as they do not encircle the city. Their purpose is mainly to protect open areas for recreation and they do allow urban growth in other directions.

Measures to restrict urban sprawl

The American planning system differs from that of many other countries since the 5th Amendment to the Constitution stipulates that the government cannot take property away from the individual without paying compensation. This includes development rights. In response metropolitan areas are using three main measures to restrict sprawl. The first is the designation of an Urban Growth Boundary – a written agreement between the city and the surrounding county that usually lasts for 20 years. Beyond these boundaries the city authority will not provide basic infrastructures such as sewerage and water or services such as fire and policing. Urban Growth Boundaries are usually employed alongside zoning measures that severely limit the density of development beyond the urban fringe to levels that are typically less than one house per ten acres. The third measure, land purchase, is discussed later in this chapter.

In Japan a Green Belt in the modern sense was first formulated in 1939 with the Tokyo Green Space Plan, only to be abandoned on the outbreak of the Second World War. Had it been implemented it would have created a protected 50-kilometre, mainly agricultural zone around the city. In the 1958 'First Capital Region Plan' a Green Belt was again proposed that referenced the 1944 Abercrombie Plan for London. The area's declared purpose was to 'control the chaotic and swollen development of (the) built up area and facilitate healthy development by creating an outer green belt'; it was to be 10 kilometres wide and beyond it would have been satellite cities.

The Green Belt was to have been implemented by local municipalities, and its failure was due largely to the absence of a powerful central authority. The Green Belt plan met with opposition from local landowners and there were no funds available for land purchase. In a rapidly growing metropolis, housing demand took precedence over the Green Belt policy and the urban area expanded into the sprawling megalopolis of today. In the end only a few small areas were protected from development. More recently the 2009 Tokyo 'Regional Plan of Metropolitan Area' has proposed a green network connecting existing waterside space and green space. However, the plan, which has not yet been accepted, lacks a concrete method for preserving green space and is unlikely to be effective.

China is adopting various forms of Green Belt to increase recreational space for urban populations, to restrict urban sprawl and to deal with pollution and water management. In its 1986 plan Beijing created two Green Belts – an inner belt of 240 square kilometres for recreation, agriculture and nature and an outer one beyond the 6th Ring Road that marks the outer edge of the city.[8] In 2017 President Xi Jinping proposed a new urban policy, 'boundaries for urban development', and subsequent guidance has required 'three control lines' (boundaries of urban development) to be designated in spatial planning strategies (Fig. 2.1). Chengdu (the capital of the Chinese province of Sichuan) had been implementing plans

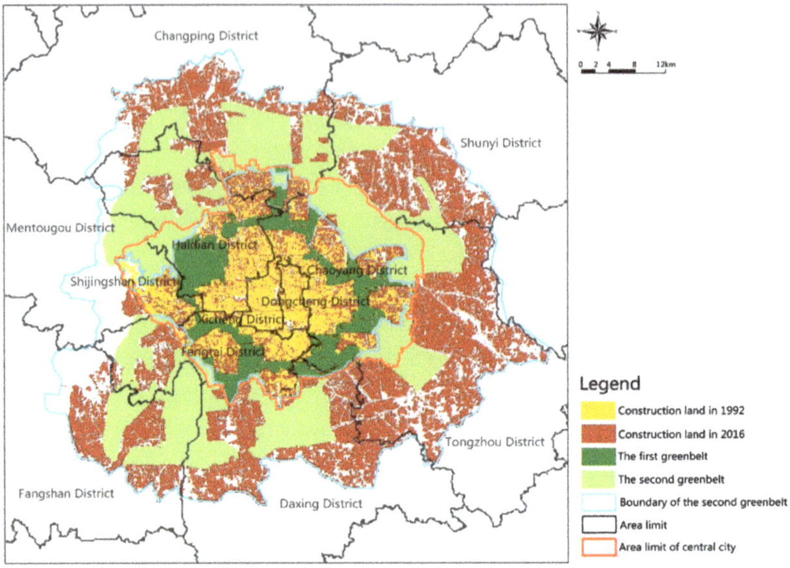

Fig. 2.1 Map of Beijing showing urban green space fragmentation and urbanisation: a spatiotemporal perspective.

Source: Li et al. 'Urban Green Space Fragmentation and Urbanization: A spatiotemporal perspective', *Forests* 10 (4) (2019): 333. CC BY 4.0.

since the 1980s for strategic green space, including the Tianfu Greenway. This will, when completed, encompass 16,900 square kilometres containing over 1,000 agricultural villages.[9] In 2018 Xi Jinping visited Chengdu and praised the parks and green spaces of *Gongyuan Chengsi* (Park City).

Metropolitan Green Belts

The post-war period saw a renewed interest in the planning for urban growth and the relationship of cities to their surrounding countryside. Chapter 1 covers the inception of the London Green Belt in the 1930s through to its formal establishment in Abercrombie's 1944 Plan for London and its subsequent expansion in the 1950s. The London Green Belt had three main purposes: to limit urban growth; to preserve the identity of individual towns; and to safeguard open land for recreational and agricultural purposes.

Green Belts with similar purposes have been incorporated into the urban planning policies of a number of German and Scandinavian cities.

These Belts are not necessarily concentric, however, as in the case of Copenhagen (see below). Outward growth in the form of corridors and urban sprawl is taking place in other areas around these cities. The most analogous European example to the UK concept of the Green Belt is the Randstad in the Netherlands. This has the same function as the London Green Belt, namely the prevention of sprawl and the protection of open countryside, but it is at the centre of a ring of cities rather than on the edge of a single metropolis. The Randstad is discussed in more detail in chapter 4.

Metropolitan Green Belts are a common policy instrument in Canada. Ottawa established a Green Belt in 1956 of 203.5 square kilometres. The area is managed by a single agency, the National Capital Commission. In Ontario, the most densely populated area of Canada, over 7,300 square kilometres of land is designated as Green Belt. In America both Portland and Seattle have Green Belts very similar in form to London and other cities in the UK. Whether or not as a consequence, these areas are also coming under pressure for new housing.

Environmental belts

Green Belts, usually in the form of belts of forest, have been used for centuries in Asia as natural barriers to mitigate against sandstorms and other climatic hazards. China in particular has a history of using landscape as a planning tool that goes back over 2,000 years. This is mainly in the form of 'greenways' along canals and city moats and drainage channels. These have evolved more recently in association with transportation corridors through tree planting along highways and railways. Greenways are also incorporated into agricultural planning for irrigation, flood mitigation and wind protection.

On a regional scale the 'Green Great Wall' project running along the northern edge of China is designed to protect agricultural land from incursions from the Gobi Desert. Recent developments in this thinking reflect changes in ideology, utilisation and scale including the use of green corridors for ecological protection and beautification. The most recent greenways in cities such as Zuhai and Guangzhou incorporate recreational activities as well as flood management and sustainable drainage measures.[10] Different strategies are key to developing the Green Belt:

> Greenways as a formative device for stitching together fragmented cities and their urbanizing hinterlands is attracting widespread

attention [...] greenways could be part of the new order, realizing the open space networks envisioned for reconnecting cities to their rural hinterland and people to nature'.[11]

The London Green Grid (chapter 3, pages 94 and 95) illustrates the development of this concept to blur the distinction of town and countryside by creating links between the two that penetrate deep into the heart of the city.

There are also new, non-urban interpretations of the term Green Belt. At the end of the Cold War in 1991 the border zones of the Iron Curtain were abandoned, along with the military facilities associated with them. The border had created an uninhabited and unfarmed zone of forests and open land colonised by many rare species. It was even unclear as to whom this area belonged. In 1989 the German Federal Agency for Nature Conservation started mapping the ecology of the border areas; it has since been designated as a 1,400-kilometre environmental corridor, the *Grunes Band Deutschland*. The initiative has been copied and developed to cover the entire ex-Iron Curtain from Norway to the Balkans. The implementation of this European Green Belt is being carried out by several hundred different agencies from the countries along its route. This is now under consideration as a UNESCO World Heritage site.

Methods of implementing Green Belts

There are two principle ways to establish a Green Belt. The first is through statutory planning powers (zoning) and the second through the purchase of the land (or development rights) by a public authority or trust. Most Green Belts are held in place through planning controls. These act to restrict development, but usually come with a set of defined exceptions where some form of development is allowed. Designation does not, therefore, guarantee preservation. Planning control has the advantage of not requiring government investment, but it requires a consistent approach and effective follow through. The example of Tokyo shows that under a weak planning system Green Belts will not survive against the pressures of urban growth. Even well-established systems such as those in London (chapter 3) and the Netherlands (chapter 4) show evidence of a slow erosion of the Green Belt.

The purchase of the development rights of land was used in the 1930s to secure Green Belt land around London. In the early parklands on the edges of cities in Australia and New Zealand the land was purchased and safeguarded in perpetuity. The UK's Garden Cities and New Towns were both based on the purchase of land to be held by the city authority or in trust. This works where land is either cheap (as it was in the UK in the early 20th century) or where all land is owned by the State (as in countries such as China). Elsewhere it is an effective but expensive way of securing Green Belt.

This method is still used by some cities in America. Here a landowner can sell or donate their right to develop land to a government agency, but the land itself remains the property of the landowner. The value is based on the difference between the market value of the property and its restricted value for farming and open space. Once agreed, a covenant is attached to the land that restricts its future use to farming or forestry. The covenant is passed to future owners and tends in practice to be permanent. Metropolitan counties in America have only been using powers to purchase or limit development rights to agricultural land since the 1970s. It is not a cheap option, however. Lancaster County in southern Pennsylvania, where many Amish live and farm, has spent more than $120 million on land and rights purchase, and the city of Lexington in Kentucky (see above) around $50 million.[12] Most schemes are funded by local government, sometimes underwritten by local taxes. There is no state role in planning at this level. Other schemes use private land trusts. Generally all three measures – agricultural zoning, Growth Boundaries and purchase agreements – are used together. This is a clever arrangement to safeguard land in the absence of a strong regulatory planning system. There have been a number of lasting successes, but in some areas restrictions to development land have led to increases in house prices above national averages.[13]

In Germany municipalities have powers to acquire land under the Federal Building Code, normally for infrastructure or flood prevention. The municipality can also acquire a plot for use according to the designations of a binding land use plan.[14] Local development plans include the open space within and beyond the city's physical boundaries and land can be purchased on the basis of 'a reasonable offer' – defined as the amount that would enable the owner to acquire an *equivalent* piece of land. This in effect means that agricultural land can be purchased by public authorities at agricultural prices.

Conclusions from Green Belt typologies

The Green Belt concept may have originated in the UK, but it has subsequently moved to many countries around the world. The drivers are to prevent sprawl and to safeguard open countryside for recreation and for agriculture and environmental aims. The concepts of Green Belts have often been adapted to fit national needs such as to limit urban growth (China), to protect nature (Canada) or to preserve farmland and give access to nature (America). The UK model is unusual inasmuch as it has combined objectives to limit sprawl and to preserve the amenity of the countryside. The closest comparisons to the UK are in the USA and in the Netherlands. The Dutch approach to planning what is largely a man-made landscape focuses on long-term land management; it is explored in more detail in chapters 4 and 5. It is also clear that planning controls on their own are rarely strong enough to protect Green Belts. A mechanism that allows land purchase, especially on the German model, provides an important long-term guarantee that open land will be preserved in perpetuity.

The Green Belt and spatial urban models

The concentric city

It is no accident that the concept of the Green Belt emerged at the same time as that of the Garden City. Although different, both were reactions to issues of health, poverty and the moral standards of an urban under-class that existed in the late 19th-century city. The new profession of town planning was an opportunity to create better living and working conditions, and access to the fresh air of the countryside was viewed as an important component of this strategy.

Ebenezer Howard's Garden City model from 1902 placed a belt of open land, mainly farmland, around each settlement. When this idea was retrofitted onto existing cities such as London, the Green Belt became a concentric ring around the city periphery. Chapter 1 traces the evolution of this Green Belt from a ring less than half a mile wide, as proposed by George Pepler in 1911, to the Green Belt of today that is up to 25 miles wide. The common element is that the Green Belt is a concentric ring around the city that has the express objective of limiting its outward growth *in any direction.*

The Garden City and the suburb are profoundly conservative (and English) constructs. The Modern movement challenged many of these concepts. Le Corbusier's 1930 *Ville Radieuse* was an attempt to articulate modernist thinking into an actual plan that incorporated the car. It introduced the concept of 'use zoning' in which the central zone was reserved for commercial land uses; outer zones were reserved for residential areas connected by carefully segregated systems of mass transportation (railways, roads and footways). Le Corbusier expanded these ideas in 1967.[15] Here he deliberately built upwards to allow the provision of parks and open spaces *within* the urban fabric. Although the *Ville Radieuse* remained a concept, its ideas were applied in the development of Brasilia (Brazil) in 1960 by Lucio Costa and Oscar Niemeyer, and in Chandigarh (India) by Le Corbusier.

Peter Hall divides urban thinkers into the 'Anglo-American and Continental European groups'. He expands on this classification:

> Nevertheless, by the 1920s and 1930s there was a rapid growth of single-family housing around all American cities, served by public transport and then, increasingly, by the private car. This was a tradition which, by and large, writers and thinkers in both Britain and the United States accepted as a starting point. On the continent it was quite otherwise. As cities grew rapidly under the impact of industrialisation and movement from the countryside, generally over several decades (the equivalent process had taken place in Britain i.e. from about 1840 to 1900) and failed to spread out to anything like the same extent [...] The typical Continental city consisted then, and still consists today, of high apartment blocks – four, five or six storeys high – built continuously along the streets, and thus enclosing a internal space within the street block.[16]

The Urban Task Force was set up in 1997 by the newly elected Labour government and was chaired by Richard Rogers. Its key recommendations promoted the idea of the 'compact city' as opposed to the model of the dispersed suburban city region. This reflected the situation in many European cities including Barcelona. Ildenfonso Cerda's 1859 plan for the *Exaimple* of Barcelona, for example, widened and extended the existing historic core to create a high-density, mixed-use city built around wide boulevards. This was part of a centrally-led programme developed in the 19th century in Spain and directed from Madrid by Royal Decree (an act of legislation that forces different cities to implement a plan). Similar plans were developed in other Spanish cities such as Madrid Plan Castro (1852) and in Bilbao by architects Alzola, Achúcarro and Hoffmeyer (1876), Valencia and Palma. *Ensanche* in Spanish means to widen and all these Plans were based on the concept that Haussmann developed for Paris.

Richard Rogers' upbringing in Florence, his family connections to Milan and Aldo Rossi, his knowledge of European urbanism and his work in Barcelona had profoundly influenced his thinking. His was an urbanism focused on the city and its citizens. The Urban Task Force's work resulted in a radical shift in emphasis from the dispersed models of growth that had dominated the post-war period to a reappraisal of urban life within the compact city. It proposed policies to bring people back to the city centre, to develop mixed-used neighbourhoods based on social and humanist principles, to pursue sustainable forms of transportation and to create open spaces *within* the city. It also advocated the reuse of brownfield land rather than building on greenfield sites in the countryside.

While this thinking supported the maintenance of the Green Belt, the rationale behind it was very different. It was driven by neither a sense of nostalgia for the countryside nor by a fear of the city. The Task Force celebrated urban living and sought to create the conditions for cities to flourish in an age beyond the private car. Its attack was on suburbia, which it saw as essentially anti-urban. Here the Task Force was questioning the suburban living and satellite New Towns of post-war planning. It believed that urban growth could be contained within existing urban boundaries, and that this was a good thing.

The work of the Task Force had critics, in particular Peter Hall. He disagreed with some of the findings in the report, stating that 'there is no overriding need to save greenfield land, of which we have a surplus in South East England; the case on sustainability grounds for further raising minimum densities is non-proven'.[17] Hall believed that there was not enough brownfield land to meet the future needs for housing. This remains a critical part of the debate on the future of the Green Belt – can the demand for affordable housing in London be accommodated within the city limits or do those limits need to be moved ever outwards?

Peter Hall had been influenced by Howard's ideal of the Garden City. His book, *The Containment of Urban England*,[18] concluded that the planning system had 'contained' urban growth in Britain and that urban sprawl associated with American cities had been largely avoided. The downside of this had been a growing housing shortage that, in his view, could not be resolved through the reuse of brownfield land within a compact city. In response, he proposed the integration of land use and transport systems to create a regional web of interconnected settlements. In a later study of urban development and regional planning in Western Europe he argued that cities were no longer homogeneous structures. Instead they were becoming constellations of smaller towns and cities, forming a wider swathe of polycentric urbanisation – particularly in Western Europe.[19]

Hall's thoughts on urban extensions as a way of accommodating growth were incorporated into URBED's winning submission for the 2014 Wolfson Prize for a Garden City.[20] This submission proposed the extension of an existing settlement to provide a new settlement of 200,000 people that would be divided into four neighbourhoods of 50,000, each with a secondary school and three primary schools. These in turn would be divided into a series of smaller neighbourhoods of 10,000, able to support a small retail centre and local employment. The model proposed a form of 'betterment tax', with the land being acquired for near to existing used value (Green Belt) and then being vested in a public foundation. The proposal was based on Dutch and German systems that allow the value generated by development to be invested back into infrastructure. Primary legislation was proposed in the form of a 'Garden Cities Act' to enable this. The case for a form of land value capture was based on the conclusion that both physical and social infrastructure needed to be in place at the beginning of development and would therefore require subsidy.

The alternative approaches of Hall and Rogers illustrate two very different spatial models for the city. Rogers' compact city is a dense area with a clear boundary that might (or might not) be designated Green Belt. Rogers' city incorporates open space within it that is accessible to the urban population. Much of the support for the Green Belt comes from its benefits for recreation and food production. However, its role in preventing outward growth, and thus creating the conditions for brownfield land to be reused and for the city to densify, is extremely important. Hall's dispersed model makes the assumption that growth cannot be contained on brownfield land and must therefore be accommodated elsewhere. He supports the role of the Green Belt in preventing sprawl, but considers that there is no significant shortage of land. He proposes the creation of satellite cities (including the growth of existing cities), very much along the lines of Howard's original model. Implicit in Hall's argument is that Green Belt can, in certain circumstances, be released for housing development.

The debate between the alternatives of the compact and the dispersed city is not just a technical one. Another important factor is the lack of affordability of housing in the UK, particularly in the city centres. The resultant increase in house prices is fuelling gentrification and the displacement of those who can no longer afford to live in the city. This 'social cleansing' will have a long-term impact on the quality of civic life. It is contrary to the principles of the European city and good urbanism. According to Aldo Rossi, a city is developed over time and a compatibility of uses and memory are key ingredients of successful cities. So too is a broad social mix. When people are forced out of the city it has profound urban, social and political implications.

One of the key drivers behind arguments for a revision of the Green Belt around London and other cities is the need to accommodate growth. Urban growth cannot, however, be separated from arguments that concern social welfare, and adequate housing should be viewed as a basic right. Social polarisation is taking place in the UK, a phenomenon contrary to the traditions of the European city where interwoven layers of poor and rich inhabitants live in proximity to one another.

These are key issues for the urbanist. The debate about the future form and function of the Green Belt is not an economic one, nor is it a technical one. It is a debate that is deeply enmeshed in the politics of the city. A two-bedroom house costs today over one million pounds in some areas of London. Perhaps that is the lens through which we should view the debate about the Green Belt?

The linear city

The urban corridor approach had been developed in Arturo Soria y Mata's *Ciudad Lineal* in Madrid (1895–1910). This replaced the traditional idea of the city as a centre and a periphery with the idea of a linear city based on connected systems of infrastructure. This concept was in stark contrast to the concentric diagrams of Howard and others in the same period. Soria's linear city used infrastructure routes as a basis for controlled expansion of the city, a rational process that would eventually join one growing city to the next. This was a radical alternative to outward growth (sprawl). The linear city was meant to 'ruralize the city and urbanize the countryside'. An important part of the project was to use tram infrastructure to connect Madrid's city centre with its outer edges and eventually to other cities. This project offers important insights into how the Green Belt could be rethought today in the UK. Implicit in the *Lineal* was the creation of good quality housing for both rich and poor in integrated, mixed-use communities.

The project, which was only partially constructed, gives an interesting insight into the edge and the growth of the city at that time. Arturo Soria y Mata asks:

> What is the Linear City? [...] the first neighbourhood of the Linear City would be composed by a 40-metre wide street, 5.200 metres in length from the Road of Aragon until Pinar de Chamartin, and an

> electric tram that runs throughout it and connects it with Madrid, arriving from one side to Las Ventas, and from the other to Cuatro Caminos [...] the inhabitants of the Linear City, and also the thousands of neighbours from Madrid that wish to spend a day in the country breathing fresh air in a leisure environment, comfortable and nice.[21]

This demonstrates concepts that embody the same thinking as the Green Belt pioneers, but it is expressed in a very different spatial form. An important part of the *Ciudad Lineal* was the incorporation of green buffer spaces in the urban fabric, designed to give spatial identity to each of the settlements. These important design elements created natural breaks in the city that distinguished one neighbourhood from another.

The *Ciudad Lineal* provided people with the chance to have a house out of the city centre and offered residents from the centre the opportunity to enjoy a day in the country. More important is the fact that the *Ciudad Lineal* utilised infrastructure and housing as essential elements of the plan. The infrastructure connected all these elements with the centre and the periphery of the city and allowed the edge to expand even further into the regional territory. In consequence inhabitants of the linear city would enjoy a different relationship with the countryside as distances would be shorter than for those living near the centre of a concentric city. The *Lineal* was a precursor to the 'Five Finger Plan' for Copenhagen (Fig. 2.5). In the original publicity brochure of the scheme (Fig. 2.2) Arturo Soria describes his vision:

> The need for fresh air in the hot summer nights, the fun in the open air, the establishment of many industries next to an important consumer centre like Madrid, and the affordable life of 'The Linear City' for the middle and working classes.

He goes on to note that there are:

> abundant sources of income that would make this project one of the most lucrative ones and a lot of people will take their money and their savings into this as it offers more security to them than the State.[22]

This statement has similarities to Howard's vision, except that the model is unashamedly urban. There are three interesting aspects about this text. The first is the fact that the periphery includes both industrial uses and cheap housing for the working and middle classes. Second, a central part of the concept was to give access to the countryside. Third, it is underpinned by a development model that gives the infrastructure companies an opportunity to invest in development and therefore maximise returns on their capital.

This relationship between infrastructure and the growth of the city may be seen elsewhere, especially in London at the end of the 19th century.

> It has long been recognised that transport services played an important part among the general influences on suburban growth [...] a much more complicated statement about the relationship between transport and development emerges from the close analysis of railway promotions and train services in outer west London, and here it is possible to see the interdependence of the two, with the promotion of new lines in advance of suburban housing both by speculative land owners and the railway company.[23]

The linear city was 'a private real estate venture that urbanised the then eastern outskirts' (see Figs 2.2, 2.3 and 2.4 below).[24]

The influence of the plan is clear in today's periphery:

> Its legacy marks the Gran Sur proposal of the 1980s put forth by the by the regional government of Madrid and is clearly visible in the main road axis of the Gran Sur (Highway M50). It is a modern-day linear city extending across six towns. The Gran Sur replaced Soria's single-family lots with office parks and subdivisions, reflecting contemporary scales and technologies.[25]

The Gran Sur is a modern version of Soria's *Ciudad Lineal*, but on a far bigger scale, extending across six towns. It shows the influence of the *Ciudad Lineal* in Madrid's modern planning, both in following a linear city approach and in using infrastructure to connect these linear axes. Peter Hall writes in regard to *Ciudad Lineal*:

> Furthermore, it can respond automatically to the need for further growth, by simple addition at the far end; it does not need to operate through restrictive greenbelts, as Ebenezer Howard's finite garden has to, so it is not surprising that the form has often appeared in regional plans as the most obvious alternative to the Howard–Abercrombie tradition.[26]

A city based on growth corridors is in fact more flexible than one with a concentric green belt. Soria's linear city (Fig. 2.2) offers important lessons on flexibility for further urban growth, particularly in its emphasis on transport infrastructure as a key element of making the corridor work. Copenhagen's 'Five Finger Plan', developed in 1947 by Steen Eiler Rasmussen and Christian Erhardt 'Peter' Bredsdorff, is a completely different spatial interpretation of Abercrombie's 1944 London Plan. The Copenhagen Plan proposed growth corridors along metropolitan train lines with green spaces in between. This created a set of linear corridors that spread outwards from the city centre like fingers from the palm of a hand. In between them, the open nature of the countryside is safeguarded. Spatially this has many advantages. It makes efficient use of transport infrastructure and gives shorter distances for the population of the 'fingers' to access the countryside. The proximity of the countryside is also likely to be more efficient in offsetting urban heat island effects.

Other cities in different countries have developed similar strategies to reconnect different parts of the city using the corridor as an urban tool to stitch together different parts of the city. Johannesburg is the economic hub of South Africa, the biggest city in the country and the centre of the Gauteng region where most of the country's GDP is generated. In South Africa an Integrated Development Plan is required under the 2000 Municipal Systems Act. One of the components of this spatial development framework is the identification of the 'Urban Edge', beyond which urban development would be severely limited or restricted. The concept was first used in Natal in the regional plans for Durban and Pietermaritzburg where it was termed 'the Urban Fence'. For a country emerging from apartheid, urban planning has a very different perspective from other parts of the world. Matters of urban growth, densification and spatial form have to be placed in the political context of how cities that had been planned to enforce racial divides can become more equitable and ethnically mixed.

Simone discusses the idea of people in the African city as infrastructure:

> But people as infrastructure describes a tentative and often precarious process of remaking the inner city, especially now that the policies and economies that once moored it to the surrounding city have mostly worn away. In many respects, the inner city has been 'let go' and forced to reweave its connections with the larger world by making the most of its limited means.[27]

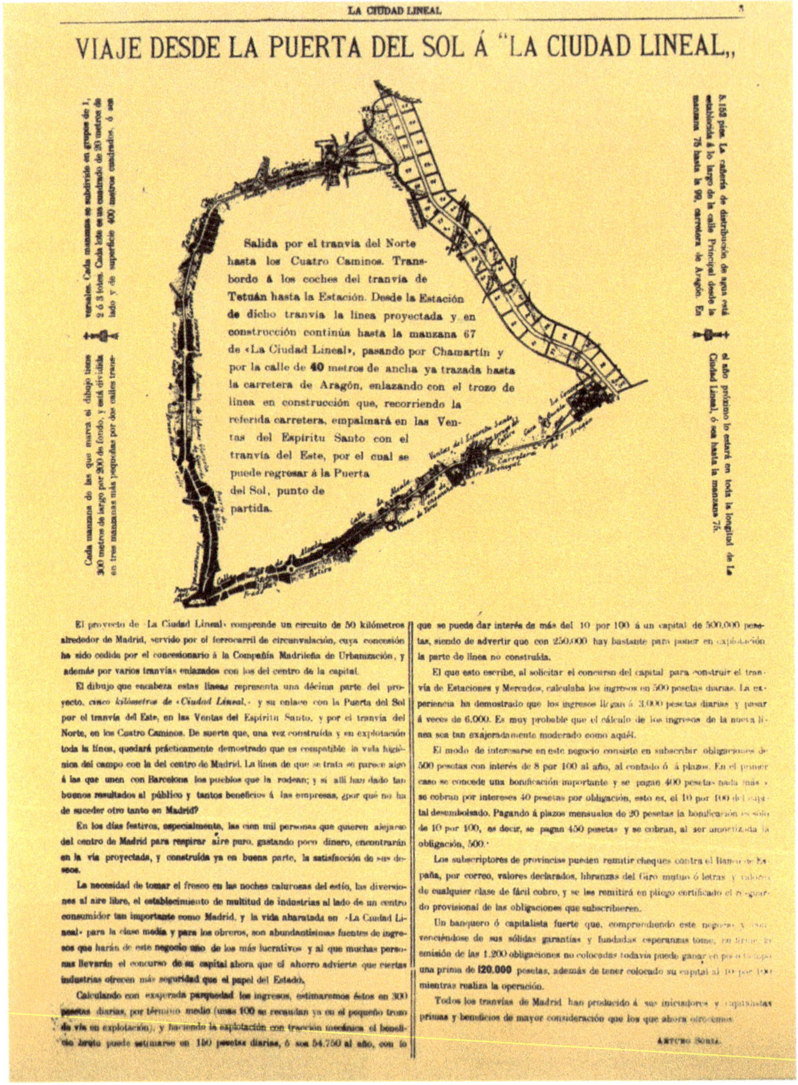

Fig. 2.2 Publicity brochure for *Ciudad Lineal*, 1911, written by Arturo Soria.

Source: 'La Ciudad Lineal'. In *Madrid (Spain: Region). Los planes de ordenación urbana de Madrid,* 3rd ed., corr. y aumentada, 29–30. Madrid: Dirección General de Urbanismo y Planificación Regional, Consejería de Medio Ambiente y Ordenación del Territorio, Comunidad de Madrid, 2006.

Fig. 2.3 (left to right, top to bottom): 1. House for a working-class family; 2. Grocery store; 3. Maria Teresa school for girls; 4. A typical affordable house, 1911.

Source: 'La Ciudad Lineal'. In *Madrid (Spain: Region). Los planes de ordenación urbana de Madrid,* 3rd ed., corr. y aumentada, 29–30. Madrid: Dirección General de Urbanismo y Planificación Regional, Consejería de Medio Ambiente y Ordenación del Territorio, Comunidad de Madrid, 2006.

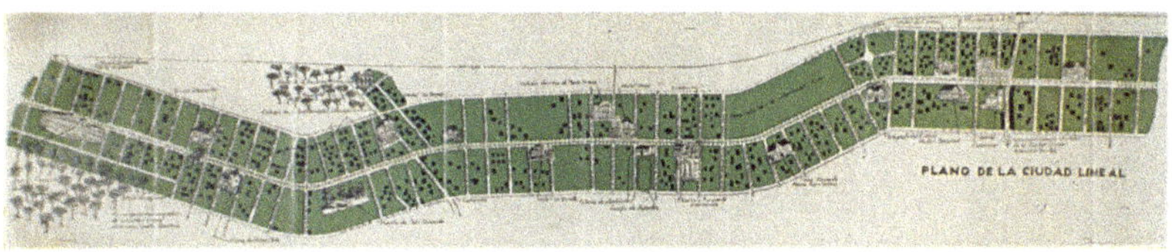

Fig. 2.4 Original plan of the *Ciudad Lineal* showing different Garden City housing typologies and green areas connected by the tram infrastructure.

Source: 'La Ciudad Lineal'. In *Madrid (Spain: Region). Los planes de ordenación urbana de Madrid,* 3rd ed., corr. y aumentada, 29–30. Madrid: Dirección General de Urbanismo y Planificación Regional, Consejería de Medio Ambiente y Ordenación del Territorio, Comunidad de Madrid, 2006.

Fig. 2.5 'Five Finger Plan' for Copenhagen, 1947.

Source: Copenhagen Regional Planning Offices. *Draft Proposal for a Regional Plan for Greater Copenhagen*. Copenhagen: Copenhagen Regional Planning Offices, 1947.

Johannesburg was polarised by the policy of apartheid into districts of different races (white, coloured and black); the white in the Central District and the black in the Townships outside the city. The Group Areas Act Policy in 1952 forced the removal of non-white people from the inner-city edge, displacing them into the outskirts of the city. The idea of the township denied people the right even to seek the opportunity to work outside of the mines. The white settlement in the centre was reserved for the privileged ruling white class. Today the white population has moved out into gated communities, as Simone writes:

> Under apartheid, Johannesburg was designed as a cosmopolitan, European city in Africa, but only for a small segment of its population. When this truncated cosmopolitanism could no longer be enforced by a white minority regime, whites fled to distant northern suburbs and gated communities where cosmopolitanism was precluded, thus leaving the inner city open to habitation of all kinds.[28]

The business district once inhabited by whites is now an informal city where other Africans, from other countries, live and settle in informal ways, seeking opportunities in the 'City of Gold'.

Apartheid had left Johannesburg a divided and flawed city in which European urban theories are of little help. Today Johannesburg is a modern metropolis with pressures of population growth fuelled by net inward migration. After so many years of apartheid rule society has become fragmented; deep-seated poverty, inequality and criminal activity have led to the development of gated communities separating rich and poor. One of the main spatial responses to Johannesburg's growth has been the adoption of growth corridors centred on public transport. The idea of the corridor formed around transit-oriented development increases the density near the corridor and gives access to public transport and economic opportunities to all citizens. As stated in the government's Spatial Development Framework:

> The Corridors of Freedom programme is the leading edge of the compact polycentricity approach that must fundamentally alter the spatial form and sustainability of the City. Public transportation is the backbone on which the new city will be constructed. It serves a dual purpose of moving people and as structuring element for mixed use intensification.[29]

This spatial model embraces the idea of development along corridors stretching out from the city centre to the urban edge and into the countryside (precisely what the London Green Belt set out to avoid). Implicit in this is the fact that the countryside is not a place to be protected from development, but an area for controlled expansion of the city based on the efficient utilisation of infrastructure. Public transportation systems also fulfil social and environmental goals. In some ways the resultant spatial form of the city is similar to the concept of 'green fingers' that underpin the plan for Copenhagen.

The Corridors of Freedom project marks a significant departure from the concept of informality that exists in many examples of urbanisation across Africa. Bremner writes in relation to Johannesburg:

> The restructuring of the economy and increasing political pressure had resulted in a city whose economic base was declining and in which the social and economic exclusion upon which it had been built was no longer sustainable. This resulted in successive attempts by the urban authorities to reinvent a city which could claim a position in the mainstream global economy and become a city all its citizens could feel part of.[30]

In this critical affirmation of post-1990's Johannesburg, Bremner mentions a city in economic decline, but suggests that in order to reinvent the city its citizens should be at the heart of the process. The Corridors of Freedom project is key in using the concept of an infrastructure corridor to reconnect and restitch different parts of the city back together. Communities are not just mere recipients of the project, but an integral part of it. The transport corridor is centred around the social infrastructure that Simone has discussed as an inherent part of the African metropolis.

This is a fascinating example of spatial form being derived from a political programme whose purpose is to reunite communities around new settlements (60 per cent of Europeans now live in this area). It is a planned urban expansion that specifically seeks to break the models of segregation once deeply embedded in the morphology of the city. Open countryside is safeguarded beyond the edge of the corridor, but the growth dynamic is linear along the transport route. The result is in effect a series of suburbs, joined by a public transit system and set within a wider (and safeguarded) regional landscape. This is the realisation of Soria's urban ideas over a century later.

The concept of the linear city has been considered by some as a possible spatial response to London's Green Belt. An LSE report[31] has examined the Green Belt around London and suggested that the concept could be used for future growth (Fig. 2.6). Their contention is that some of the land designated as Green Belt is in fact of indifferent quality, and that

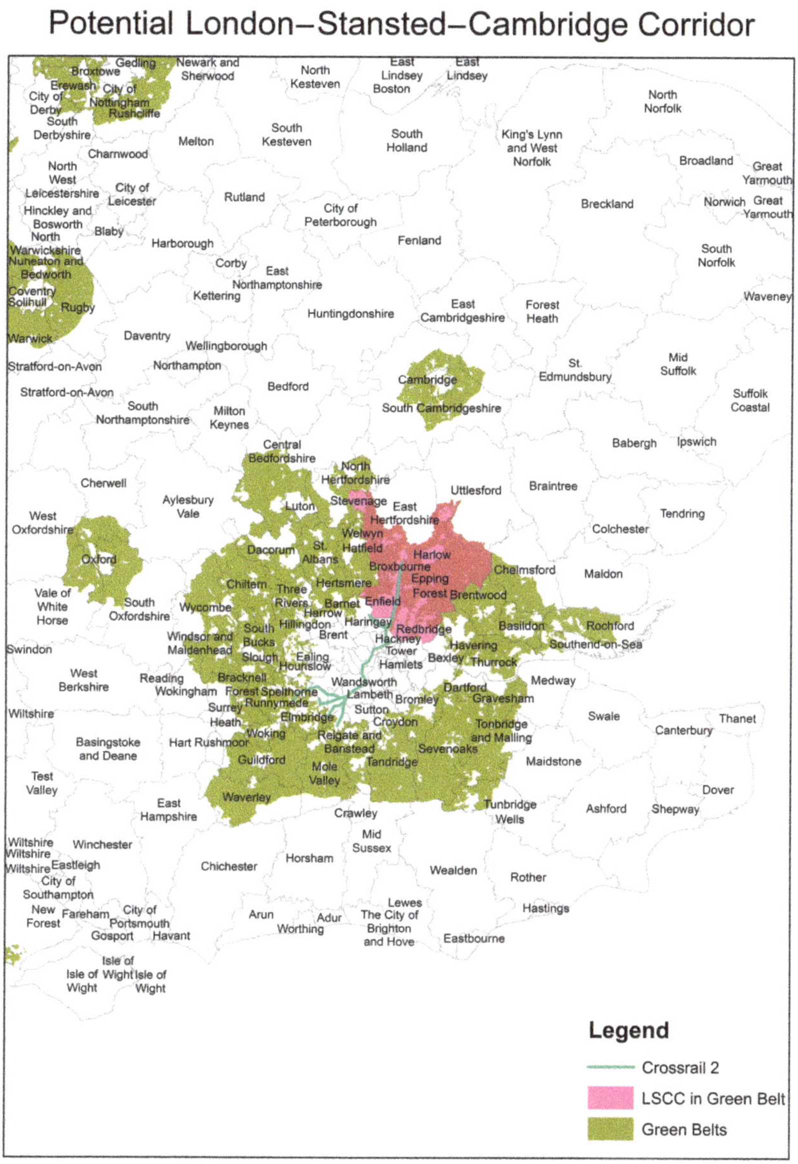

Fig. 2.6 Proposal for a linear city connecting London and Cambridge, 2016.

Source: Mace et al. *A 21st Century Metropolitan Green Belt*. London: LSE, 2016, drawing on DCLG. *Area of Designated Green Belt Land*. London Data Store, 2015; McGarva, G. *GB Transportation Network (1:50 000 Meridian 2)*. Edina ShareGeo Open, 2010; UK Data Service – Census Support. English Districts, UAs and London Boroughs, 2011 (Generalised).

the Belt's present extent is stifling growth and contributing to regional housing shortages. The report suggests that there might be opportunities for parts of the Green Belt to be developed, under specific criteria, along growth corridors. It proposes corridors similar to the Copenhagen plan and the *Ciudad Lineal*, arguing:

> The wedges/corridor approach holds special potential for Metropolitan Green Belt reform, in both the long and short term. We suggest that an effective way to kick-start change would be to introduce an initiative in one of the city region's dynamic coordination corridors that should act as a stimulus to develop a new approach to Green Belt policy.

It describes the proposals as Green Belt 'topiary' that would implicitly enhance the recreational and ecological value of the green wedges around each corridor. Sites of Special Scientific Interest and Areas of Outstanding Natural Beauty would be preserved from any development. The proposal would result in a corridor connecting Central London to Cambridge via the Upper Lea Valley and Stansted Airport. This would require amending the National Planning Policy Framework (NPPF), but the corridor could be implemented by local authorities along its route.

The unrestricted city

There is, of course, another model – one that allows the unrestricted growth of the city. In many ways this would be the very antithesis of the Green Belt as it would license urban sprawl. Lerup defines sprawl around American cities:

> In sprawl, units, swatches, zones, and domains come to the fore [...] the observer can read through the trees for the hundreds of thousands of houses, the meandering streets, the cul-de-sacs, the arteries and the continuous freeways [...] The orientation of the house ... (makes no regard to) ... the compass, the landscape, or prevailing ecology. Inefficient and wasteful, sprawl's true power and success lie in its economic and social effectiveness.[32]

This definition of American sprawl produces a clear image of the American landscape, in which hundreds of houses are scattered around the outside of the city in cul-de-sacs that are inward-looking and dependant on the car.

> In the North America city, it is the centre, a territory comprised of the 'downtown' and adjacent neighbourhoods, which historically has been associated with the marginal [...] the city is the space of the devil incarnate. The periphery, principally the 'suburbs', are 'Paradise regained'.[33]

This is the complete opposite of the compact European city.

The area at the edge of the town is often uncontrolled and poor, without rules or legislation. The European city's edge is not the place where 'Paradise is regained'. It is the centre, where the middle and upper classes live, that is usually considered one of the wealthiest areas. In Madrid the centre is not associated with decline; historically it is the edge of the city that is referred to as *extrarradio* ('outside of the radius'). Herein lies one of the most significant differences between the UK and European city. In the former suburban areas often 'leapfrogged' an inner ring of industry to establish wealthy neighbourhoods for those fleeing the depressed 'inner-city' areas of cities. This gave rise to a situation similar to that of American cities in which a wealthy core is separated from the periphery by a concentric band of deprived neighbourhoods. The proximity of wealthy districts to the urban fringe is one of the factors behind the desire to preserve the Green Belt.

In modern Spain development is occurring on the urban periphery. It is largely driven by speculation (either public or private), and a construction boom has fuelled the outward growth of the edge of many Spanish cities. Two pieces of legislation promoted such expansion. The first was the Boyer Decree (1985) that liberalised the market and allowed the owners of second homes to rent their properties freely. The second, the Ley del Suelo (1998), promoted by the Conservative government of President Aznar, allowed agricultural land to be turned into building land and simplified the planning process into three uses for the land: *urbano* (urban land), *urbanizable* (land that can be urbanised) and *no urbanizable* (land that is not possible to be urbanised). Neuman comments:

> Every 20 years or so since 1920 Madrid has undergone a city planning cycle in which a plan was prepared, adopted by law, and implemented by a new institution. This preparation–adoption–institutionalization sequence (and the planning institutions that support it) have persisted – without exception – despite frequent upheavals in society.[34]

There is a strong relationship between the Boyer Decree and what we see in Madrid today, as Fernando Roch explains:

> This Decree promoted the expansion of the middle-class suburb, the destruction of the territory, the overdevelopment of the infrastructure, the functional segregation that accentuated the opposition centre-periphery [...] giving a great impulse to today's dispersed models and acts as a catalyst of the real estate boom of the late eighties.[35]

There are alternatives to this, however. Advances in telecommunications may not be making the need for face to face contact redundant, but they are changing the dynamics of location. This does open up the possibility of more dispersed spatial models where the urban edge becomes blurred. The Dutch model (chapter 4) of a managed landscape that contains layers of infrastructure and settlement set within a landscape offers an alternative pattern of settlement. The logical conclusion from the Dutch model would be an 'urban field' where landscape penetrates into the city and the city extends into the countryside. This would be a highly planned and managed spatial form that is subservient to its regional landscape. This concept is developed further in chapter 5.

Conclusions

The Green Belt ideal has been surprisingly resilient over the past hundred years. It has been passed between countries and adapted to suit local circumstances. Green Belts may be categorised as peri-urban parklands, mechanisms to control growth, composite metropolitan Green Belts and environmental buffer zones. In reality, many fulfil a range of these functions. A conclusion that may be drawn from the success – or otherwise – of Green Belts is that a range of measures are required to counter development pressures and thus to avoid their slow erosion. A strong planning regime, especially where there is long-term policy certainty, is the core measure. This also needs to be backed up by land purchase schemes. The American Urban Growth Boundaries are particularly interesting as a means of limiting sprawl. Why, after all, should society foot the bill for low-density speculative development on the urban periphery? Land purchase schemes similar to those in the 1930s in England (see chapter 1) are now too expensive to be a feasible policy option, unless coupled to measures to acquire at agricultural values. In this respect the German public purchase scheme is of particular interest. After all, the Garden City Movement assumed that land would be purchased at agricultural values (the Letchworth Garden City Trust still owns most of the town), as did the New Towns.

The Urban Task Force Report was a seminal moment in British planning. Richard Rogers' preferred model of the compact city looked to continental Europe for answers to urban problems. The idea of a dense, mixed use and socially diverse city that was based on sustainable transport (walking and cycling) and proximity to open spaces was in complete contrast to the traditions of post-war spatial planning advocated by planners such as Peter Hall. Hall's model of the dispersed city can be traced directly back to Howard and the Garden City Movement. The New Towns appeared brave experiments, but were in reality vehicles for population overspill. They might have made sense in a time when large industrial zones needed a skilled or semi-skilled labour force close to the factory gates, but this was no longer the condition of the UK in the late 20th century. The compact city anticipated the rise of globalisation, the high, value-added creative economy and more sustainable models of living. The Garden City might have been an interesting concept at the beginning of the 20th century, but by the end it was well past its sell-by date.

A compact city might, however, take different forms. The UK model of the concentric city sitting inside a Green Belt or Green Girdle should be compared to European models of the linear city. Arturo Soria's *Ciudad Lineal* proposal for Madrid, the 'Corridors of Freedom' in Johannesburg and the 'Five Finger Plan' for Copenhagen are powerful alternative spatial models. They allow dense residential/mixed use development to take place along corridors that radiate out from the city centre. This overcomes the problems of outer suburbs that are not dense enough to support viable public transport systems. It also means that more of the population live within easy reach of the amenity of the countryside. The device of breaking these 'fingers' with landscape buffers, as proposed by Arturo Soria, prevents the problem of cities coalescing with one another along transport routes. The proposition from academics at the LSE for a series of growth corridors from London to cities such as Cambridge are interesting and worth further consideration.

The story of the Green Belt is not over; it may be about to begin again. The move by the Chinese government to limit urban sprawl within clearly defined boundaries shows that the concept is still relevant over a hundred years later. It is too early to judge this initiative, but it will almost certainly spawn new variations on what is a very familiar theme. There are different options for the future of the Green Belt that do not destroy it, but rather accommodate it in a different relationship with the city. In the context of rapid and potentially disastrous climate change, the Green Belt offers a reservoir of potential. International best practice might allow all of this thinking to develop into a single sustainable model that also includes environmental stewardship of the land.

Author's note

IN MEMORIAM

This chapter is dedicated to the life and memory of my grandmother, Mrs Adela Ruiz Aja (1930–2020), who brought me up.

Este capítulo está dedicado a la vida y memoria de mi abuela Doña Adela Ruiz Aja (1930–2020) que me educo y con la que crecí.

Notes

1. Kühn 2003, 20.
2. Hall 2002, 31.
3. Lynch 1960, 576.
4. Solà-Morales i Rubió 2008.
5. Hebbert 2006.
6. Delhi's Forest Ridges were designated in 1857 and landscaped in 1912. Mumbai's Sanjay Gandhi National Park was designated in 1945 as the Krishnagiri National Park and Chennai's Guindy National Park in 1958.
7. In 2019 the city voted to preserve its Green Belt despite development pressure from a city that had increased sevenfold in size during the intervening period.
8. Wu 2015.
9. Kuo 2019.
10. Known as the 'Sponge City' initiative.
11. Walmsley 1995, 81.
12. Daniels 2010.
13. Daniels 2010.
14. Voss 2010.
15. Le Corbusier 1967.
16. Hall 2002, 27.
17. Rogers et al. 2005.
18. Hall et al. 1973.
19. Hall and Pain 2006.
20. URBED 2014.
21. Soria 2006, 26.
22. Soria 2006, 30.
23. Thompson 1982.
24. Neuman 2010, 97.
25. Neuman 2010, 97.
26. Hall 2002, 45.
27. Simone 2004.
28. Simone 2004.
29. City of Johannesburg 2016.
30. Bremner 2000, 184.
31. Mace et al. 2016.
32. Lerup 2000.
33. Woodroffe et al. 1994.
34. Neuman 2010.
35. Roch 2004.

References

Boeri, S. *L'anticittà*, 1st ed. Rome: Laterza, 2011, 29–30.

Bremner, L. 'Reinventing the Johannesburg Inner City', *Cities* 17 (2000): 185–93. https://doi.org/10.1016/S0264-2751(00)00013-5.

City of Johannesburg Metropolitan Municipality. *Spatial Development Framework 2040*. City of Johannesburg: Department of Development Planning, 2016. http://www.parkview.org.za/docs/townplanning/Johannesburg%20Spatial%20Development%20Framework%202040.pdf. Accessed 28 February 2020.

Daniels, T. L. 'The Use of Green Belts to Control Sprawl in the United States', *Planning Practice & Research* 25 (2) (2010): 255–71. https://doi.org/10.1080/02697451003740288.

Hall, P. *Urban and Regional Planning*, 4th ed. London, New York: Routledge, 2002.

Hall, P., Gracey, H., Drewett, R. and Thomas, R. *The Containment of Urban England* (two vols). London: Allen and Unwin 1973.

Hall, P. and Pain, K. *The Polycentric Metropolis: Learning from mega-city regions in Europe*. London: Earthscan, 2006.

Hebbert, Michael. 'Town Planning versus Urbanismo', *Planning Perspectives* 21 (3) (2006), 233–51. https://doi.org/10.1080/02665430600731153.

Kühn, M. 'Greenbelt and Green Heart: Separating and integrating landscapes in European city regions', *Landscape and Urban Planning* 64 (1–2) (2003): 19–27. https://doi.org/10.1016/S0169-2046(02)00198-6.

Kuo, L. 'Inside Chengdu: Can China's version of the megacity work?' *The Guardian*, 4 February 2019. Accessed 4 February 2019.

Le Corbusier. *The City of Tomorrow and its Planning*. New York: Dover Publications, 1967.

Lerup, L. *After the City*. Cambridge: The MIT Press, 2000, 53–4.

Li, F., Zheng, W., Wang, Y., Liang, J., Xie, S., Guo, S., Li, X. and Yu, C. 'Urban Green Space Fragmentation and Urbanization: A spatiotemporal perspective', *Forests* 10 (4) (2019): 333. https://doi.org/10.3390/f10040333

Lynch, K. 'The City Image and its Elements'. In *The City Reader*, edited by T.R. Le Gates and F. Stout, Routledge Urban Reader Series, 5th ed., 576. London, New York: Routledge, 2015.

Mace, A., Blanc, F., Gordon, I. and Scanlon, K. *A 21st Century Metropolitan Green Belt*. London: LSE, 2016. http://eprints.lse.ac.uk/id/eprint/68012.

Neuman, M. *The Imaginative Institution: Planning and governance in Madrid*. Farnham, Surrey; Burlington, VT: Ashgate, 2010.

Roch, F. *Agentes Sociales y tendencia urbanísticas: hegemonía inmobiliaria y perdida de urbanindad*. In *Urbanismo en el siglo XXI: una visión crítica: Bilbao, Madrid, Valencia, Barcelona*, 1st ed., edited by J. Borja, Z. Muxí and J. Cenicacelaya, 88. Barcelona: Escola Tècnica Superior d'Arquitectura de Barcelona: Edicions UPC., 2004. Author's translation.

Rogers, R. et al. *Towards a Strong Urban Renaissance*. Urban Task Force, IPPR, 2005. http://image.guardian.co.uk/sys-files/Society/documents/2005/11/22/UTF_final_report.pdf.

Rossi, A. and Eisenman, P. *The Architecture of the City*. Published for the Graham Foundation for Advanced Studies in the Fine Arts, Chicago, Illinois and The Institute for Architecture and Urban Studies, New York, New York. Cambridge, MA: The MIT Press, 1982 (rev. ed. 1984).

Simone, Abdou Maliqalim. 'People as Infrastructure: Intersecting fragments in Johannesburg', *Public Culture* 16 (3) (2004): 407–29. Project MUSE. https://muse.jhu.edu/article/173743.

Solà-Morales i Rubió, M. de. *Las formas de crecimiento urbano*. Barcelona: UPC, 2008.

Soria y Mata, A. 'La Ciudad Lineal'. In *Madrid (Spain: Region). Los planes de ordenación urbana de Madrid*, 3rd ed., corr. y aumentada. Madrid: Dirección General de Urbanismo y Planificación Regional, Consejería de Medio Ambiente y Ordenación del Territorio, Comunidad de Madrid, 2006. Author's translation. Please note that this text is a summary of the original text 'Datos acerca de la Ciudad Lineal', Compañia Madrileña de Urbanizacion, 1911, translated in English as 'Details about the Linear City', Madrid Urbanisation Company, 1911.

Thompson, F.M.L. 'The Case Against the Historical Inevitability of Suburbs'. In *The European Cities and Technology Reader: Industrial to post-industrial city*, edited by D.C. Goodman, 35–6. London; New York: Routledge, in association with the Open University, 1999 [1982].

URBED, Uxcester Garden City. *Second Stage Submission for the 2014 Wolfson Economics Prize*, August 2014. https://policyexchange.org.uk/wolfson-economics-prize-2014/.

US Bureau of the Census. 'Population Estimates and Projections' (press release). Washington DC: US Bureau of the Census, 14 August 2008. Available at www.census.gov (cited by Daniels 2010).

Voss, Winrich. *Compulsory Purchase in Poland, Norway and Germany – Part Germany (4220).* Fig. XXIV. International Congress 2010. 'Facing the Challenges – Building the Capacity.' Sydney, Australia, 11–16 April 2010. https://www.fig.net/resources/proceedings/fig_proceedings/fig2010/papers/ts03f/ts03f_voss_4220.pdf. Accessed 2 March 2020.

Walmsley, J., A. 'Greenways and the Making of Urban Form', *Landscape and Urban Planning* 33 (1995): 81–127. https://doi.org/10.1016/0169-2046(95)02015-L.

Woodroffe, J., Papa, D. and MacBurnie, I. 'An Introduction'. In *The Periphery*, edited by M. Toy. London: Architectural Design, 1994, 7.

Wu, Nawei. 'An Introduction and Comparative Study of the Implementation Approaches of Beijing's Green Belts'. In *Proceedings*, 8th Conf. Int. Forum Urban, C006. 2015. https://doi.org/10.3390/ifou-C006. Accessed 4 February 2019.

Chapter 3
An arena of conflict: the Green Belt debate in the 21st century

Peter Bishop

Introduction

The Green Belt is probably the UK's best known and most popular planning policy. It has successfully limited the outward growth of cities and largely prevented ribbon development along the major transport arteries. The restrictions on outward growth have been an important factor in concentrating investment back into inner urban areas through recycling brownfield land. If traffic congestion has not entirely been averted, then at least the nightmare scenario of widespread low-density, car-dependent suburbs has been avoided. In this respect Green Belt policies have not only protected the countryside, but have also contributed to the broader objectives of environmental sustainability. A compact city is a far more sustainable model for living than are low-density, car-reliant suburbs. The London Metropolitan Green Belt now comprises 153,860 hectares of land covering parts of London and eight adjacent counties (Fig. 3.1).[1]

However, there is a growing recognition among some planners, developers and politicians that Green Belt policy is having unintended consequences. As the need for land for housing to accommodate a growing population meets resistance from rural communities anxious to preserve the amenity of their areas, it is becoming a contentious policy. Is the Green Belt beginning to strangle the growth of the city? Is preserving the amenity of more prosperous communities in the countryside condemning many in the poorer sections of society to live in over-dense and unsatisfactory conditions? Has housing now become so unaffordable

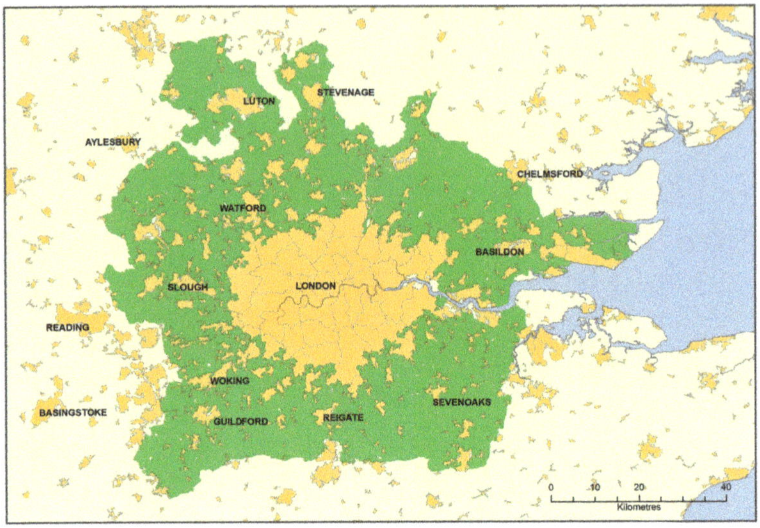

Fig. 3.1 Map of the London Metropolitan Green Belt, 2010.

Source: All Party Parliamentary Group for London's Green Belt, CPRE/ London Green Belt Council, APPG for London's Green Belt 2019.

in the UK that the prospect of home ownership is beyond the reach of many?

No policy can withstand the winds of change. And change is occurring rapidly, on numerous fronts. Since 1951 the population of the UK has increased by around 40 per cent and car ownership by 14 times. During this period society's needs and expectations have also altered beyond recognition. The consequences of climate change are raising entirely new questions around the interrelationship between cities and their regions, urban resilience and the role of Green Belt. Government pledges to reduce carbon emissions drastically can only be credible with radical rethinking of the ways in which city regions function.

Too often, the current policy debate is simplified into polar positions: on one hand to preserve the Green Belt as it is, on the other to relax the policy to accommodate housing and urban growth. For some, the Green Belt is sacrosanct and any 'nibbling away' is a highly emotive prospect. Yet those demanding a structured release of Green Belt also make broad assumptions about housing need that ignore the realities of supply, location and tenure. In both options the issues are far more complex than a narrow focus on the release of land for development. The current policy debate needs to reflect this complexity. For example, what is the role of Green Belt in relation to the critical issues of climate change and environmental sustainability? Who pays for infrastructure if the city is to expand? If land is released on the periphery of the city, how can this ensure the provision of affordable housing and public space where they are most needed? Is a system where the re-designation of Green Belt land results in huge windfalls to owners really the best way of resolving urban growth? A new policy debate is long overdue.

Section 1 of this chapter provides an overview of the current context within which Green Belt policy is operating. It examines housing development pressures and arguments that are being made for the release of Green Belt or a relaxation of policies. It then considers whether there is evidence that the Green Belt is being lost and explores the political battles that are taking place to protect it. It concludes with an assessment of current government policy. Section 2 considers whether there might be an alternative approach to thinking about the Green Belt and its future. It looks at the condition of the urban fringe and highlights two case studies that have examined opportunities for accommodating new development on the urban edge. This chapter concludes with an examination of the ways in which planning policy operates, along with its implications for land values. In this context it considers options for the capture of land value increases that arise from the grant of planning permissions for new housing. The conclusions in Section 3 consider the options for alternative approaches to the Green Belt and its future operation.

Section 1: An overview of the Green Belt: pressures and policy

Housing pressures and the Green Belt

The shortage of housing at affordable prices in the right locations in England is beyond dispute. While between 1959 and 1988 around 7.5 million houses were built, the total dropped to just 3.3 million between 1988 and 2016. This fall is despite a growing population, more and smaller households and demands for higher standards of individual space. The problem caused by the restriction of new housing is illustrated by the ratio of median household income to median house prices. For England this stood at 3.84 in 1996, but in 2018 it had reached 7.8. In some areas it is considerably higher: Cambridge (12.95) and parts of London (15.54).[2] The Barker Review of Housing Supply, commissioned by the

UK Treasury, concluded that an *additional* 70,000 houses per annum would be required just to reduce increases in real house prices from 2.4 per cent to 1.8 per cent.[3] However, a report by the National Audit Office in 2019 showed that supply was well below the government's target of 300,000 a year.[4] Between 2005–6 and 2017–18 an average of 177,000 new homes per year have been built; the number has never exceeded 224,000. To meet its declared target the government would need a 69 per cent increase in the average number of new homes built since 2005–6.[5]

Population growth in London between 1997 and 2016 has resulted in an acute housing shortage giving an assessed shortfall across the capital of 700,000 houses.[6] The unavoidable conclusion is that either commuting or overcrowding is increasing – probably both. The 2013 London Strategic Housing Market Assessment (SHMA) identified a need for 49,000 new homes each year,[7] yet between 2013–14 and 2016–17 just 33,000 homes a year were built. The new 2017 SHMA, published alongside the draft London Plan, found that London now needs 66,000 new homes a year. On top of this, of course, land is needed for new schools, hospitals and other facilities, as well as for open space. Despite the growing pressures to deliver new housing, the Mayor has dismissed proposals to weaken Green Belt policies around London.

The reasons for the national shortfall in supply are complex. They can be traced back (at least) to changes in government policy in the 1980s that first reduced the direct provision of new social housing and subsequently removed any direct grant subsidy for affordable housing. Targets of around 300,000 houses a year have not been achieved since the mid-1970s, and then only when local authorities were major providers.[8] The private sector has averaged considerably less than 200,000 houses a year since the mid-1970s. The housing supply crisis triggered a government review (Barker, K., HMSO 2004) chaired by economist Kate Barker. The situation continued to worsen and, revisiting the the issue in 2014, Barker observed:

> The number of homes built in England from 2010 to 2013 was less than half the official estimate of how many more households would want to find somewhere to live.[9]

The housing market is also distorted by a range of other factors including under-occupation, overcrowding and involuntary sharing, second homes, buy to let and overseas investment. Housing has become an investment and a tradable commodity. The market is also sectoral with different regional demands and a chronic lack of genuinely affordable housing in locations of the highest demand and need. Ultimately there is a finite supply of brownfield land within cities for housing, and as a result urban housing densities are being pushed to unsustainable levels. The question is whether the relaxation of Green Belt land is the answer.

Arguments for Green Belt release

Over the last decade or so, the worsening housing crisis has stimulated growing calls from a wide spectrum of interests for a review of Green Belt policy – mainly for residential development. In one report the Social Market Foundation Commission stated that it will be impossible to build all new housing on brownfield sites, meaning that 'a significant proportion (of new housing) will need to be accommodated on greenfield sites'. It argued that there was a case for reconsidering the future of the Green Belt, which 'often protects neither wildlife nor areas of outstanding beauty'.[10] The National Federation of Builders (NFB) has also called for a reassessment of Green Belt boundaries.[11]

In January 2015 the Adam Smith Institute released a paper questioning the value of Green Belts, describing them as 'not the bucolic idylls that some imagine them to be'.[12] It stated that over one-third of Green Belt was devoted to intensive farming (with net environmental costs) and compared the Green Belt on the urban edge as 'indistinguishable from what many understand urban sprawl to be'. The paper argued that there were substantial social costs associated with maintaining the Green Belt, in particular high business costs and volatile house prices. It proposed the abolition of the Green Belt as a move to solve the housing crisis – or, failing that, the release of land within a 10-minute walk of main line commuter railway stations. This, it claimed, would provide one million additional houses. Another paper, published by Freer, a Conservative thinktank, similarly proposed relaxing rules on building homes within half a mile of railway stations, as these are areas that likely to be in 'high demand' which are already well served by transport links.[13]

Urban Architecture advocated in 2015 that the Green Belt should be used for development to avoid the average house price for London reaching 'a million pounds by 2020'. It inferred that while some parts of the Green Belt are indeed Sites of Special Scientific Interest (SSSI), Areas of Outstanding Natural Beauty and Heritage Coasts, these were protected by other forms of planning legislation. The remaining areas of Green Belt, they argued, should be considered for development.[14]

Such arguments are apparently finding support from some politicians. In 2018 it was reported that a majority of Theresa May's

Cabinet supported more radical measures, such as liberalising planning laws and relaxing Green Belt restrictions, to help tackle the housing crisis.[15] In an interview in 2019 with *The Times* the Conservative MP Jacob Rees Mogg accepted that an element of Green Belt development would be necessary in order to provide enough new homes (with gardens).[16] His rationale was that not all Green Belt land was in areas of Outstanding Natural Beauty.

These and a number of similar reports essentially rest on arguments that the housing crisis is a supply side problem and that the Green Belt is a reservoir of undeveloped land of mixed amenity value, which if released would result in reduced house prices. However, the assumption is that demand is flexible, that the optimum location for new housing is outside the city and that infrastructure will be provided, presumably by the state. Even proposals to develop just around existing stations assumes that capacity exists in the rail system, a fact that many commuters would dispute. Many of the policy papers that point to the dubious agricultural or ecological value of the Green Belt lack sufficient support from current research.

While accepting that releasing planning restrictions on Green Belt would increase housing supply (and theoretically reduce land prices), it is a leap too far to suggest that there is a direct relationship between the existence of Green Belt land and the shortage of housing in England. The relaxation of policy on the Green Belt is unlikely to address the imbalances in the housing market. Without other policy interventions or programmes, affordable housing is unlikely to be provided at the levels required or in the right locations. The realities of the housing crisis are rather more complex than simply increasing the supply of land, and so too should be the policy responses.

Part of the argument for Green Belt release is that local residents are likely to support the construction of new local homes. For instance, a survey by the Centre for Policy Studies found that 47 per cent of people believed that 'while most of the countryside around England's towns and cities should be protected, some ought to be used for new housing and other development'. Those aged between 25 and 34 were particularly likely to support new homes being built locally.[17] A citizens' jury organised by the business lobbyists London First decided overwhelmingly in favour of Green Belt review:

> We came to that decision as a group as we realised that there is a terrible crisis for housing in London and that there is a big need for affordable and social housing for the people that live in London.[18]

On the basis of this work London First suggest that 'genuinely green belt' should be protected, but that decisions should be made locally concerning the release of low-grade land, including rubbish dumps and construction sites. Such surveys are being used by think-tanks and professionals as evidence that attachment to the notion of the Green Belt is decreasing.

In the absence of any definitive research, however, it is difficult to assess just how strong public opinion is. People may indeed be willing to entertain housing in the Green Belt – as long as the development does not occur in their backyard. There does appear to be a gulf between *strategic* public opinion, which recognises the need for more housing, and *local* opinion, which will resist proposals in their particular locality.

The growing concern over climate change, the importance of the natural environment and the number of endangered species are factors that have not yet been added to this complex debate nor attracted much research. Yet public support for responsible environmental policies is becoming an increasingly powerful concern.[19] Most people, if asked, would probably claim to favour better housing at affordable prices – but if this was at the cost of the destruction of the natural environment, their decision might be different. Local opposition has always been counted in terms of votes, but the growing profile of groups such as Extinction Rebellion suggests that the loss of open space and habitats is becoming a higher priority for the public. A survey carried out in 2016 by Ipsos/Mori and the CPRE showed a high level of support for the Green Belt, particularly among those aged 25–35 where 60 per cent of respondents supported the retention of the Green Belt. The policy debate over the Green Belt's future is certainly more complex than partial surveys or citizens' juries would suggest.

Erosion of the Green Belt – fact or fiction?

Concern over the loss of open countryside has persisted since the 19th century. In 1928 Clough Williams-Ellis published a book, *England and the Octopus*, to coincide with the establishment of the Campaign to Protect Rural England (CPRE). The book's cover shows the tentacles of the urban 'octopus' strangling the English countryside. Its Preface includes a reprint of a cartoon from the satirical magazine *Punch* that captured the popular mood. It shows Mr Smith leaving his village in 1914 to go to war (to preserve his native soil), only to return four years later to find it engulfed and unrecognisable as an urban dystopia. The writer J.B. Priestley, on a tour of England in 1933, was clearly appalled by the sprawl of new roads and suburbs; he commented 'We might suddenly have rolled into California'.[20] This sense of an inexorable loss of the countryside persists today.

Green Belt land is indeed being eroded (Table 3.1). In the five-year period between 2008/9 and 2013/14 the total loss of Green Belt amounted to 1,040 hectares – around 0.6 per cent of the total.[21] More recently the loss of Green Belt has increased.[22] There was a decrease of 3,290 hectares (0.2 per cent) in the area of Green Belt between 31 March 2018 and 31 March 2019. The extent of the designated Green Belt in England as at 31 March 2019 was estimated at 1,621,150 hectares, around 12.4 per cent of the land area of England. Although Green Belt loss appears to have been relatively small, it is a cumulative process. In the five-year period from 2013/14 there was an approximate loss of 1.1 per cent of Green Belt in England (0.3 per cent in the London area). At this rate it would take 250 years for the currently designated Green Belt in England to disappear completely. That might seem to be a remote possibility, but it is worth remembering that the Green Belt has been in place for almost 90 years and represents a legacy that once lost can never be replaced.

Although the actual loss of Green Belt might be small, there is evidence that the development *threat* to the Green Belt is beginning to accelerate. Local authorities, under pressure from central government to deliver more housing, have been given housing targets that they are expected to deliver through their Local Plans.

The CPRE was one of the early proponents of the Green Belt and has campaigned ever since for its extension and protection. It argues strongly that housing needs can be met by repurposing brownfield land. Indeed, where studies of land availability have been carried out, they tend to support the contention that there is sufficient land available within urban areas to accommodate new housing requirements for the foreseeable future.

An analysis by the CPRE in 2018 found that more than 12,350 acres were cut from England's Green Belts by redrawing boundaries in 2017, a loss of 0.3 per cent.[23] The CPRE reported in 2018/19 that the number of residential applications on greenfield sites in the Green Belt was the highest it had ever been, and would result in 27,308 additional housing units. Maidment (2018) reports that England's Green Belt suffered its biggest reduction in eight years with more than 5,000 hectares lost as councils across England removed protections on land to meet government housing targets.[24]

The CPRE has become increasingly critical of the pressures that local authorities face from central government to include Green Belt land

Table 3.1 The distribution of Green Belt designated land by region of England: 2009–14

Region	2009 area (hectares)	2010 area (hectares)	2011 area (hectares)	2012 area (hectares)	2013 area (hectares)	2014 area (hectares)
East/London/ South East	580,410	580,730	580,690	580,460	580,570	580,380
East Midlands	78,620	78,930	78,930	78,930	78,950	78,950
North East	72,990	72,990	72,990	73,040	73,060	73,060
North West	262,730	262,780	262,770	262,800	262,440	262,300
South West	110,130	110,130	110,130	110,130	110,620	110,420
West Midlands	269,380	269,380	269,380	269,340	269,360	269,360
Yorkshire and the Humber	264,580	264,640	264,640	264,680	264,290	264,290
England total	**1,638,800**	**1,639,560**	**1,639,530**	**1,639,380**	**1,639,290**	**1,638,760**

Source: DCLG, 2014.

in their development plans, despite there being considerable brownfield land available.

A report by the London Green Belt Council (LGBC)[25] in 2019[26] states:

> There appears to be no lessening of pressure on the London Green Belt for housing and this in spite of its importance for farming, recreation, climate change, flooding and a major role in health and welfare especially for those suffering from mental health symptoms, as described in the Government's report – A Green Future.[27]

The report found that 55 out of the 66 local authorities with London Green Belt land within their boundaries plan to build on the Green Belt. In the local planning authorities within the London Metropolitan Green Belt area, over 202,715 new houses were proposed. Meanwhile a total of 4,934 hectares of brownfield land was available within these planning authorities, able to accommodate at least 260,383 new homes.[28]

The number of Green Belt sites around London under threat from development increased from 203 in 2016 to 443 in 2017 and again to 519 in 2018. In the same period the number of houses proposed increased from 123,500 to 231,653 (Fig. 3.2).[29] Not all of this housing will be built, but the latent pressure identified leads the CPRE to conclude in September 2019 that:

> This is a clear indication that the Government's green belt policy to protect green belt land and *prevent urban sprawl by keeping land permanently open* is not working. The green belt is being eroded by land being taken, through the local plan process, in order to meet so-called objectively assessed need for housing.

The battle for the Green Belt

The Barker Review of Land Use Planning in 2006 considered public perceptions of the percentage of built-up areas in England.[30] Remarkably, it revealed that 10 per cent of respondents believed that 75 per cent of England was built up, and over 75 per cent of respondents believed that 25 per cent or more was developed. In reality just 9.9 per cent is developed.[31] But this misconception about our 'small overcrowded island' is a potent political force. It surfaces repeatedly – influencing, for instance, the fears about immigration that partly fuelled Brexit.

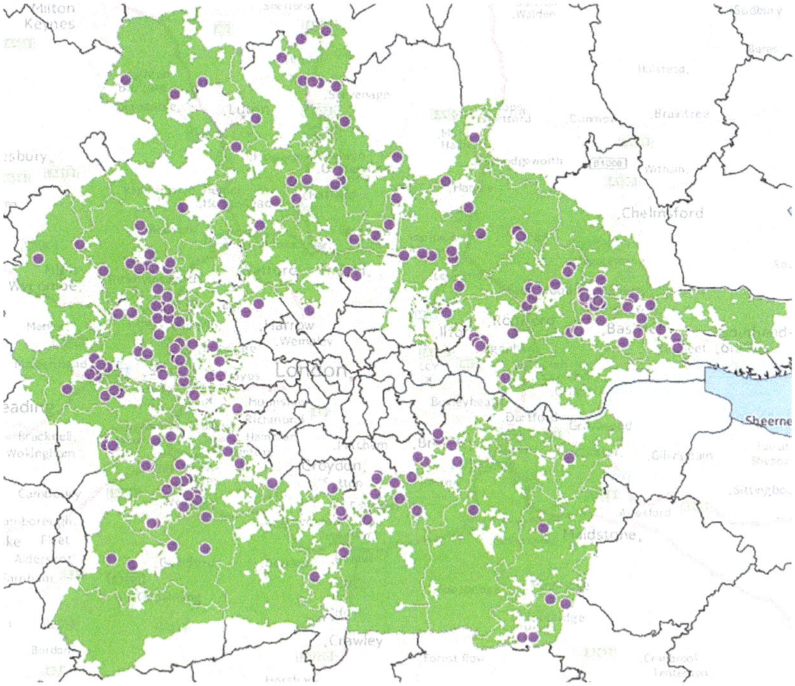

Fig. 3.2 Map showing specific threats to the London Green Belt (203 sites), July 2016.

Source: 'Safe Under Us? – Two Years On'. London Green Belt Council, January 2019, 5–6. Copyright © London Green Belt Council, 2019.

In fact the 9.9 per cent of the land that is developed is somewhat less than the 12.9 per cent of land that is designated as Green Belt.[32] The perception is weakened further when the constituent parts of the 9.9 per cent in urban areas are analysed. Across England, only 8.2 per cent of built-up areas are buildings; the rest (91.7 per cent) is 'green space', including water and unclassified uses.[33] Even within the administrative area of Greater London, the built-up area is only 27.5 per cent; green areas amount to 65 per cent, of which 23.8 per cent are domestic gardens. Public perceptions may be inaccurate, but nevertheless they represent a level of anxiety that is having an impact on politics and therefore on policy makers.

Despite figures revealing that the loss of Green Belt to development is less than 0.2 per cent a year, there is growing public concern that the Green Belt is under threat. New houses on what was once greenfield land are highly visible (and who knows who might come and live in them!). The idea of developing Green Belt is therefore politically contentious. It also makes good newspaper coverage. Writing in the *Independent* newspaper under the somewhat emotive headline 'Should Britain Build on its Green Spaces to Solve its Housing Crisis?', Alister Scott outlines the issue as:

> Alterations to the green belt boundaries can only be made by local governments in exceptional circumstances ... In practice, though, it seems the criteria aren't always quite so strict. Increasingly, greenfield sites (undeveloped land, which can include the green belt) are being favoured by developers because they are cheaper to exploit than brownfield sites. [34]

A central problem with Green Belt development is that opposition is local and focused. Consequently it is not surprising that such objections often find support from local politicians. Local residents who object to development in their locality represent real votes that can be counted. The counter arguments, from those in housing need, are general and unrelated to the local debate. Their votes are purely notional and in any case some way off in the future.

The housing shortage in the UK and the resultant lack of affordability, particularly for first-time buyers, is beginning to impact on public attitudes to the Green Belt. A poll by ComRes in 2018 for the right-wing think-tank Centre for Policy Studies (CPS) found that local residents are significantly more likely to support the construction of new homes in their areas than to oppose them.[35] However, these attitudes do not necessarily translate into local support when specific proposals are brought forward.

In reality opposition from local communities that feel threatened by Green Belt development proposals appears to be growing. For example, the Cambridge Local Plan proposed 14,000 new homes, of which just 3 per cent were to be in the Green Belt. Yet this caused considerable opposition from campaign groups in 2014, who even proposed that a city centre flood-plain site occupied by a bowls club should have houses built upon it instead.[36] The debate is emotive. Writing in the *Financial Times*, Ed Hammond reported that 65 acres of 'exhaust-smudged scrub' on the outskirts of St Albans has become the battleground for a clash between ambitious developers and a community who like things 'the way they are'.[37]

Such conflicts are being repeated across the country. Eleven sites within the Green Belt around Stourbridge are currently under review for possible housing development as part of the Black Country Core Strategy Review. The Save Stourbridge Green Belt website was set up and is now run by residents to raise public awareness of threats to Stourbridge's Green Belt and to inform local residents by providing links to publicly available material. It encouraged participation in public consultations and organised petitions to the Council.[38] The Tunbridge Wells draft Local Plan, covering the period 2016–36, looked to release more than 5 per cent of the borough's Green Belt, primarily to accommodate 14,776 new homes. The draft did not designate any land to compensate for the Green Belt that was set to be lost. According to KentOnline, 'there was strong criticism of Tunbridge Wells Council when cabinet members met to consider whether to move their Local Plan process on to the next stage'.[39] The majority of complaints came from residents of Capel and Tudely who objected to the council's plan to create a 'Garden Village', which they referred to as Tudely New Town. An online petition organised by the Save Capel Campaign attracted more than 2,800 signatures and Save Capel has organised two public exhibitions to explain what is being proposed.

In the London Borough of Enfield residents are also opposing the release of Green Belt land for housing. Enfield Road Watch began life in 2015 to object to the potential development of the Crews Hill Green Belt. Their campaign involved local residents, the Enfield Society, the Western Enfield Residents Association and the CPRE. However, wider threats to the Green Belt led the action group to expand its goals and mission. It now has a supporter list of over 1,000, while more than 22,000 people have signed its petition to protect Green Belt land. The campaign group has set up a website, is encouraging responses to the Local Plan consultation and is organising public meetings and awareness raising through social media.[40]

While Conservative cabinet ministers might be willing to consider the principle of relaxation of parts of the Green Belt to ease the housing shortage, individual MPs are likely to come under pressure from their constituents – and, when they do, to seek help from their ministerial colleagues. In 2018 the Communities Secretary James Brokenshire intervened to prevent East Hertfordshire District Council from adopting its Local Plan after the local MP raised concerns from local campaigners concerning possible loss of Green Belt. The Plan's proposals would have permitted 600 new homes on a 17 hectare site.[41]

Such battles are having a significant influence on the political landscape. An analysis by the London Green Belt Council (LGBC) of the local council elections in May 2019 showed that where authorities had proposed development on Green Belt land, the ruling party had, in each case, either been voted out of office or had its majority substantially reduced.[42] The CPRE Essex reports that:

> While in other parts of England, Brexit and other national issues may have determined the course of the recent elections, it is clear that in counties such as Surrey, Berkshire, Essex and Hertfordshire, which are within the London Metropolitan Green Belt (LMGB), the outcome of district and borough councils had been influenced more by communities' anger at proposals to build housing estates on Green Belt land than by any other concern.[43]

In Surrey the swing was most striking. The Conservatives – the ruling party in most of the county's district and borough councils – lost 117 councillors (out of 1,269 national losses in total), meaning that Surrey accounted for almost 10 per cent of all Conservative losses in the 2019 May local elections. According to the LGBC, the Conservative electoral performance was worst in the three Surrey districts where the Local Plans threatened to release Green Belt land for housing: Tandridge, Guildford and Waverley. In each of these areas the Conservatives lost control of the local councils to residents' associations, local campaign groups and independent candidates, all of whom had stood on a platform to oppose the Local Plans and pledged to defend the Green Belt from development. In Guildford the newly formed Guildford and Villages Group, which stood on a platform of defending the Green Belt, won 15 seats. An existing local party, the Guildford Greenbelt Group, won an additional seat, giving them a total of four.

The Localism Act introduced by the Cameron government in 2011 promised to make the planning system more democratic and introduced neighbourhood plans to allow communities a say in where new houses should go. In practice, the well-off and the well-housed use it to resist, not promote, the development of new homes. A study by Turley of neighbourhood plans found that of 75 published neighbourhood plans, 55 per cent were designed solely to resist development. This rose to 63 per cent in rural areas, mainly Conservative electoral heartlands. Three-quarters of plans were in the south of England, where the need for housing is most acute.[44] This suggests that more prosperous districts are seeking to protect their areas from new homes and to push undesirable developments into poorer neighbourhoods.

Shortcomings of government policy

The CPRE attributes the blame for this growing threat to the Green Belt directly to the Housing White Paper. This proposes that local authorities should be expected to review Green Belt boundaries every five years and allocate more land for development if developers fail to build at the required speed. While it acknowledges that development on such land is only allowed by the NPPF under 'exceptional circumstances', the CPRE raises concerns that the planning system is too weak at a local level to resist development and that many consents are awarded on appeal.

Although Green Belt loss has hitherto been slow, there is no reason to suppose that this will be the case in the future. The UK planning process is heavily influenced by precedent, and there is a legitimate fear that if a clearly defendable policy is breached then incremental development will be harder to resist on a case by case basis. Although the *principle* of the Green Belt is not under threat, the interpretation of policy is open to change and there are clear indications that the pressures for new housing are pushing policy makers towards relaxing some of the criteria. In this respect the CPRE has argued that the 2017 Housing White Paper could serve fundamentally to weaken the status of Green Belt.[45]

Initially this appears strange, as the White Paper states that Green Belt boundaries should continue to be altered only in 'exceptional circumstances' and after all other reasonable options for meeting housing need have been 'examined fully'. However, the definition of 'exceptional circumstances' (para 1.39 of the White Paper) specifically includes 'housing requirements'. The CPRE argues that the test could be used by developers to justify a constant state of Green Belt review. This is a significant change in emphasis from previous policy statements that housing demand alone is not sufficient justification to change Green Belt boundaries. The CPRE also argues that the requirement to 'examine fully' other options may be toothless in practice. Since the introduction of the NPPF in 2012, planning inspectors have rarely challenged local authorities who have promoted Green Belt release, even where there are significant amounts of brownfield land available.

A report by Brentwood Borough Council shows that the annual rate of loss of Green Belt has doubled since the NPPF came into force in 2012:

> Green belt boundaries are now being changed to accommodate housing at the fastest rate for at least two decades. At least 800 hectares of greenfield land in the green belt have been developed for a range of commercial or industrial projects, such as offices or retail parks, since 2009. Nearly three-quarters of the housing proposed on land to be released from the green belt will be unaffordable for most people living in the local area: planning consultants Glenigan found only 16 per cent of homes built in Green Belt since 2009 were affordable. With the New Homes

Bonus,[46] the Government is providing financial incentives that significantly increase green belt release and development, contrary to its own commitments.[47]

A degree of permanence and continuity is an essential requirement in policy making. If the market senses that policy will be relaxed, development is likely to be deferred. This applies especially to Green Belts, where granting a residential consent might increase the value of the land by a factor of 250 times from its agricultural value. The CPRE argument that Green Belt boundaries, once set, should endure for at least the typical 15-year life of a development plan is difficult to refute. The White Paper, however, suggests that Green Belt boundaries should be reviewed every five years, as part of the five-yearly review of Local Plans. This is a licence for land banking and speculation.

While part of the rationale for development in the Green Belt is the need for affordable housing, most of the development that is proposed is not 'affordable'. Of the homes proposed for the Green Belt, less than 30 per cent of units were considered affordable.[48] Moreover, the average densities of new housing were around 21 dwellings per hectare (dph), compared to 32 dph outside the Green Belt (and up to well over 400 dph in parts of London).[49] If the option of developing on Green Belt around mainline stations were to be pursued – and if these new settlements were to be sufficiently sustainable to support a primary school and local services – residential densities would need to be around 100 dph.[50] Low-density development in the Green Belt represents an inefficient use of a scarce land resource. It also is likely to result in a car-based housing model with higher individual carbon footprints and traffic congestion.

Proposals to develop within 800 metres of railway stations make significant assumptions about the amenity or ecological value of the land concerned. They also miss a key point. If access to the countryside for the urban population is a primary purpose of the Green Belt, then surrounding every station that offers convenient access to the countryside with development might rather defeat that purpose.

More recently emphasis has been placed on the importance of Green Belt as a place for nature and biodiversity as well as offering some mitigation against climate change. The importance of the countryside for sustainable food production, water conservation, carbon reduction (through forestry) and ecological diversity are now major considerations. While some of the Green Belt might currently score few points against these criteria, its scores could be enhanced dramatically through careful management. Its development would permanently remove this potential for ever. The future could be an environmentally rich Green Belt with greater public access, woodlands, wetlands and natural parks. The environmental arguments for protecting the Green Belt are strengthened by the issues raised by climate change. The Green Belt of the future would also be an essential component of any strategy to ameliorate extremes of temperature, flooding and contribute to health and wellbeing.

The arguments for protecting the Green Belt are largely the same as those made for its creation over a hundred years ago. It protects the open countryside which is both beautiful and agriculturally productive, prevents urban sprawl, protects the distinctiveness of existing settlements and is a place for recreation. Most of those involved in the debate would accept all of these as being 'good things' that have tangible social value. In addition to arguments concerning the intrinsic value of the Green Belt, there are other more practical reasons for protection.

- The planning system is unable to make strategic choices as it is too fragmented at local level, weak and under resourced
- Under the present policy regime, the partial release of Green Belt is unlikely to provide sustainable or affordable housing for those in need
- If the Green Belt is to be reviewed it should be as an environmental resource, not as a means for providing houses

Section 2: Towards a new approach to the Green Belt

This section considers various elements that are required if a new approach to Green Belt policy is to be considered. It argues that given the ragged edge of the urban fringe, the mix of uses and range of urban and rural characteristics of the Green Belt and the need for suburban intensification, detailed surveys are required. It then considers the need for a National and Regional Strategic Plan to allocate uses rationally. This section concludes with a consideration of the mechanisms through which some percentage of the uplift in value that accrues through changing the designation of land can be used to contribute to the costs of providing infrastructure and ensuring that any new housing is indeed affordable.

A ragged edge

The urban edge was not the result of a conscious planning process; it was just the place where development stopped at the outbreak of the Second

World War. This boundary was subsequently frozen when the Green Belt was extended immediately after the war. On close examination, the urban edge often consists of streets that end in open land and uses that are neither urban nor rural, forming a transitional zone between the town and the countryside. These streets along with retail and industrial parks, railways and aerodromes are a random rather than a planned condition, but are now cemented by planning policy. The case study on Northolt later in this chapter illustrates this point. At best, the boundary between town and countryside is a ragged edge.

This transitional zone blurs the distinction between town and countryside. Often there is no clear-cut boundary but rather activities that span both zones – allotments in the city and businesses in the Green Belt. Some settlements on the fringe of outer London exhibit more of the characteristics of rural than urban areas, while some settlements in the Green Belt are undoubtedly more urban in character.

In January 2010 CPRE and Natural England commissioned a report that assessed Green Belt uses in England.[51] Around London it found that only 58 per cent of Green Belt land was registered as being in agricultural use (compared with 71 per cent of all land in England) and that there was a high prevalence of 'semi-urban' uses on open land, such as golf courses, paddocks and riding stables. Within the Green Belt, woodland covered 18 per cent of the overall land area. On the edge of metropolitan areas some districts are considerably more rural than urban in nature. Shepperton to the south-west of London, for example, is 65 per cent Green Belt, while Brentwood to the north-east of London is described as being 10 per cent built-up area, 8 per cent recreational area, 76 per cent agricultural and 6 per cent woodland.[52] Figures 3.3 and 3.4 show the amount of the London Metropolitan Green Belt that is designated as having particular environmental significance and open public access. In both cases the areas are relatively small.

In many places the open countryside penetrates the city as much as the city sprawls into the countryside. The London Plan has a specific category of protected open space called Metropolitan Open Land. This is almost indistinguishable from Green Belt in terms of status and protection. In 2007 Design for London produced the East London Green Grid, which in 2010 evolved into the All London Green Grid, subsequently incorporated into the London Plan (Fig. 3.5). This policy framework seeks to connect 'fingers' of open land in the urban area to the open countryside beyond the M25 and aims to form a network of linked spaces and wildlife corridors. Many areas of Metropolitan Open Land London have significant importance for recreation, food production and ecology.

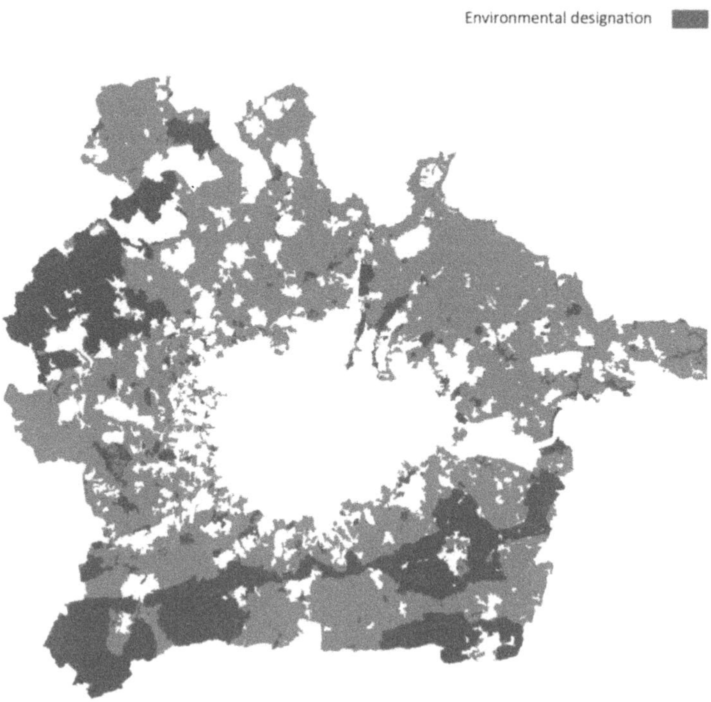

Fig. 3.3 Map showing Green Belt land which has been designated as having environmental importance, 2016.

Source: Natural England Open Data, 2016.

The London Green Grid developed ideas from the 1944 Abercrombie Plan for London, which promoted a network of publicly accessible parks and open spaces. Such strategies, dating over 70 years, demonstrate that there is no clear edge to the city; the city and the Green Belt are a single zone and should be considered as such.

The condition of the urban fringe has been examined in various academic studies, most notably by Marion Shoard.[53] She describes this urban periphery as 'edgeland' – a disorganised but often fertile hinterland between planned town and over-managed country. This landscape is part man-made and part natural, but it provides an untapped resource both for wildlife and for human exploration. These informal peripheral sites are as much a part of the broader urban economy as housing and shops. Although they might not all allow

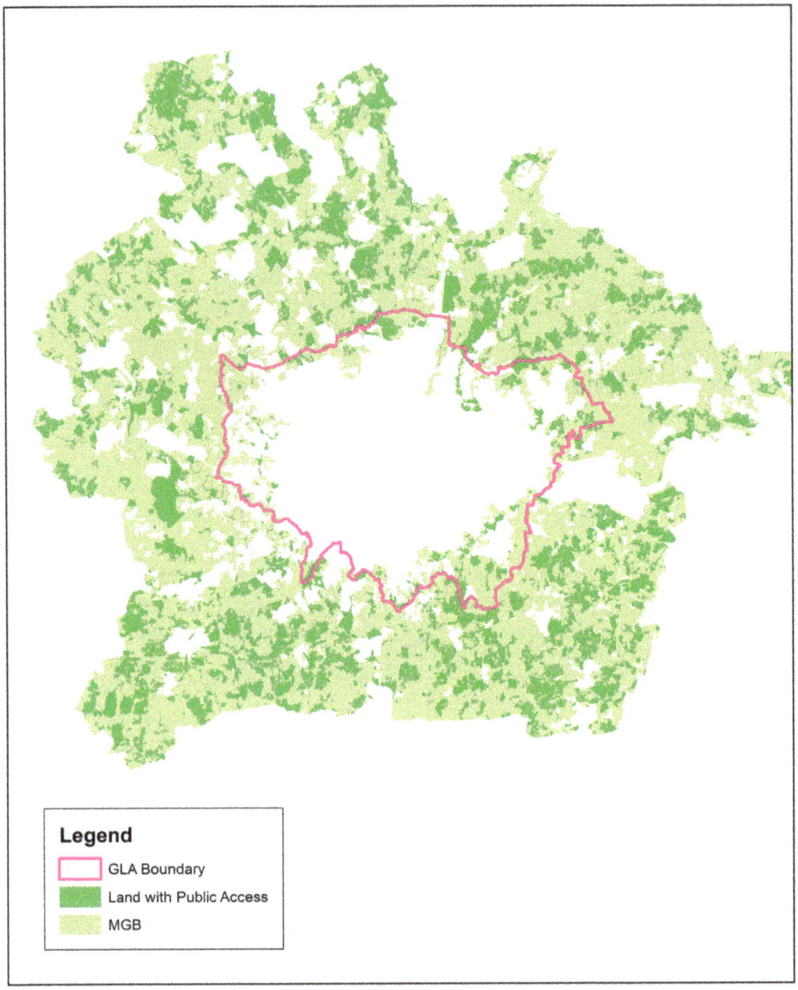

Fig. 3.4 Map showing land with public access in the whole Metropolitan Green Belt (MGB), 2016.

Source: Mace, A. et al. *A 21st Century Metropolitan Green Belt*, p.19, fig. 3. London: LSE, 2016.

general public access, some have recreational value and many have significant ecological importance. A dismissal of such landscapes under the auspices of 'tidying up' the urban edge does not represent a rigorous understanding of the important function of the urban fringe. These are the *terrains vague*; their importance has attracted many writers and practitioners who value those everyday elements

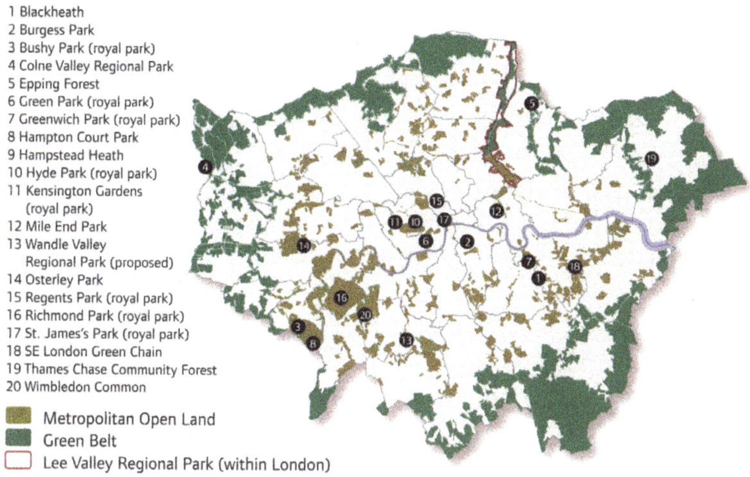

Fig. 3.5 Map showing Greater London Green Belt and Metropolitan Open Land, 2016.

Source: *The London Plan*, 2016 (GLA).

that make up the richness of city life and provide both human and ecological habitats.[54]

The debate over whether or not to release Green Belt land must carefully consider the nature of the urban fringe. It does not just concern the release of greenfield sites or the reuse of brownfield land. It must also embrace how better use can be made of the low-density outer suburbs. The concept of suburban densification has been on and off the policy agenda for a considerable period, viewed by many as desirable in theory, but ultimately dismissed as too difficult. Suburban land is mainly in highly fragmented ownerships and existing house prices usually preclude individual redevelopment. This does not mean that its potential should be dismissed by policy makers, however, especially when the default options are hyper-density or building on open land.

A recent study by Hunt Thompson Associates, *Supurbia*, advocates the densification of the outer London suburbs.[55] It calculates that there are 725,000 detached and semi-detached low-density houses where opening up parts of the gardens could provide an additional 100,000 new houses. The study also calculates that doubling the existing density of the outer London boroughs would provide one million new houses. While accepting that these are hypothetical numbers and that there are significant barriers to overcome in just releasing a proportion of this land, it does suggest that any review of the urban edge should consider a deep zone that includes the suburbs on the urban periphery.

There are a range of possible ways in which the Green Belt could be reconfigured and some of these are considered further below. Research papers published by the LSE explore a range of options from maintaining the status quo through to new settlements in the countryside and even complete abolition.[56] The papers also consider a spatial rethink of the Green Belt in the form of growth corridors and 'green wedges', such as the idea of a London–Stansted–Cambridge corridor, and make a set of specific design and planning propositions.[57] The Centre for Cities argues for release of land within 800 metres of railway stations with a maximum 45-minute journey time of the centre of the five major cities in England (excluding any land of amenity or environmental value).[58] It argues that this could provide 47,000 hectares of housing land and would increase the supply of new housing by between 7 and 9 per cent. The total loss of Green Belt would be around 1.8 per cent. The London Society, which was instrumental in creating the Green Belt, commissioned research that concluded there is a 'need to move away from the idea that the countryside is a sacrosanct patchwork of medieval hedgerows' and towards the recognition of 'housing as a need to be met in locations with appropriate environmental capacity'.[59]

London First, an organisation that represents business in the capital, argues that the lack of affordable housing is now one of the main concerns of business and that brownfield land alone cannot accommodate London's growth.[60] The London First report concluded that:

> London must continue to protect its valuable green spaces and beautiful open countryside, but this is wholly compatible with seeing how the green belt can play a small part in helping to accommodate the new homes that London needs. London's boroughs should be encouraged to review their green belt and consider how the land within it can be most effectively used and what the options are for re-designating a small fraction for new homes.

This ignores the fact that the majority of the Green Belt is outside London's metropolitan boundaries.

Any case for the release of Green Belt for housing needs to focus on a qualitative assessment of Green Belt land, site by site in specific areas. The case study of Enfield (below) illustrates one way forward.

Case study of Enfield: an assessment of development opportunities

The London Borough of Enfield is on the western edge of London and contains a significant amount of Green Belt land. Development for new housing was proposed in the Council's latest Local Plan document. Some 37 per cent of Enfield is designated Green Belt land but, with a new homes target of 1,876 a year, the Council's draft Local Plan proposed a fresh look at Green Belt boundaries. The Local Plan options included the release of between 5 and 10 per cent of Green Belt land for new family housing, in particular land around Crews Hill station – only 30 minutes from King's Cross. The main existing use of this land was horticultural nurseries and garden centres.[61] Interestingly the draft Local Plan did not consider the release of Strategic Industrial Land (SIL). Although this is protected under the London Plan, so too is Green Belt.

In response to this the Enfield Society and CPRE London published a detailed survey of the London Borough of Enfield to identify a range of large and small sites that might provide space for new housing.[62] The sites were selected on the criteria that they currently made poor use of space and could be intensified and put to better use. The research demonstrated there is theoretically space to build at least 37,000 homes on previously developed land (PDL) in Enfield, without the need to build on Green Belt. This would represent 10 years supply at the current GLA targets for the borough (which the report authors considered in any case to be at least 30 per cent too high).

The study identified alternative development options. The main proposals focused on two areas where there were concentrations of retail warehousing and low-density industrial parks. In the Southbury area the study suggested that an intensification of the area around the station might yield 15,271 new houses and that the development on industrial land at Ponders End would yield another 2,500 units. Similarly, the intensification of land around Lower Edmonton, currently in similar retail use, could provide another 10,000 houses. A survey of micro sites carried out at the same time identified a further 510 possible sites comprising 480 hectares of land that might be suitable for housing. Allowing for the fact that not all of these sites would be suitable, the study concluded that even if 30 per cent were to be developed a further 1,953 houses could be developed in the borough without encroaching onto Green Belt land.

Case study of Northolt: a planned reassessment of the Green Belt

In 2016 the London Borough of Ealing and Catalyst Housing Association commissioned Allies and Morrison to carry out an assessment of part of London's urban fringe in Northolt.[63] The brief was to appraise the clients' land holdings and review the quality and development potential (if any) of the surrounding Green Belt and Metropolitan Open Land (MOL).

Northolt is typical of many areas of outer London. Having been a cluster of small farming settlements in the 19th century, it grew rapidly on the back of new bus and rail transport systems. Development was largely halted by the outbreak of the Second World War. The designation of London's Green Belt in 1955 then effectively froze the area in time with streets that had been partially developed becoming dead ends. In many ways the Northolt area remains an 'unfinished project'. Residential densities at 40–45 units per hectare are below the London average and hamper the provision of efficient transport and local services. The Northolt area has large areas of both Green Belt and MOL, although surveys show that there is little discernible difference between land in the two designations. The Green Belt around Northolt consists of a mixture of parks, farmland, private leisure, golf courses, mineral extraction and open countryside. A relatively low percentage of land allows direct open public access.

The study mapped and analysed the Green Belt and MOL to assess its accessibility, environmental function, intrinsic landscape quality and character (Figs 3.6, 3.7, 3.8, 3.9 and 3.10). It found a significant range in the quality and value of the land – some areas had very high recreational and ecological value, but others, such as mineral extraction sites and golf courses, had little. While there was a very important chain of connected landscapes around the canal and watercourses, other areas of Green Belt were not connected and were not part of a coherent urban landscape. In terms of flood mitigation and water quality, however, much of the open land played an important role in rain and storm water drainage, particularly along the Yeading Valley. Finally a subjective assessment of landscapes was carried out using site visits and photography (Fig. 3.10).

The various criteria were then amalgamated into a composite plan to provide an overall assessment of the Green Belt and MOL landscape (Fig. 3.11). This identified sizeable areas of Green Belt and MOL that were significantly underperforming and where either development or

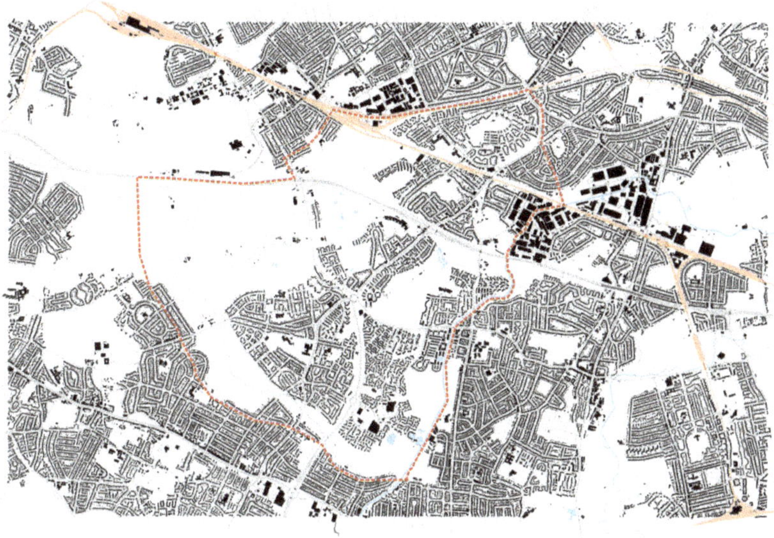

Fig. 3.6 Street map showing Northolt (north-west London): a suburb frozen in time, 2016.

Source: London Borough of Ealing/Allies and Morrison. *Northolt Framework*. Allies and Morrison, 2017.

Fig. 3.7 Plan showing the Green Belt and Metropolitan Open Land (MOL) around Northolt, 2016.

Source: London Borough of Ealing/Allies and Morrison, 2016. *Northolt Framework*. Allies and Morrison, May 2017.

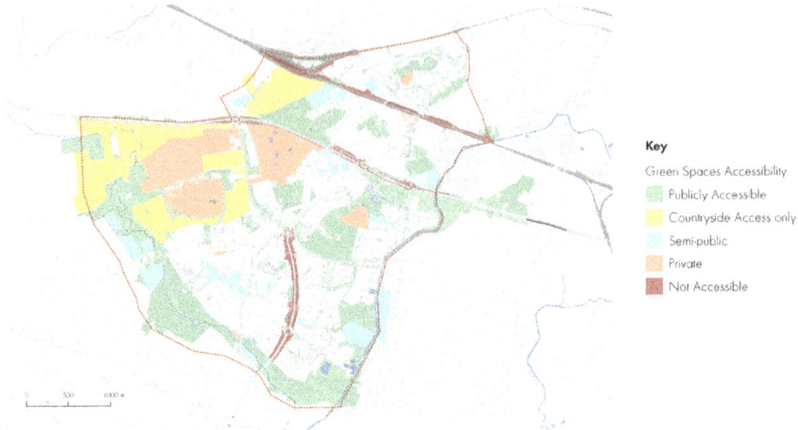

Fig. 3.8 Map showing public access to open land around Northolt, 2016.

Source: London Borough of Ealing/Allies and Morrison. *Northolt Framework*. Allies and Morrison, May 2017.

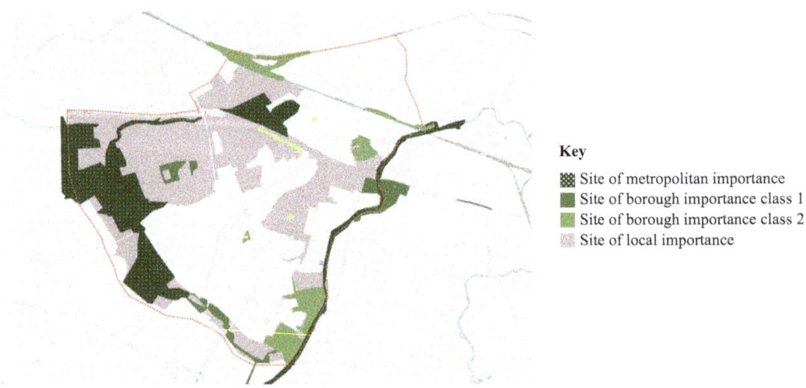

Fig. 3.9 Map showing the nature conservation value of open land around Northolt, 2016.

Source: London Borough of Ealing/Allies and Morrison. *Northolt Framework*. Allies and Morrison, May 2017.

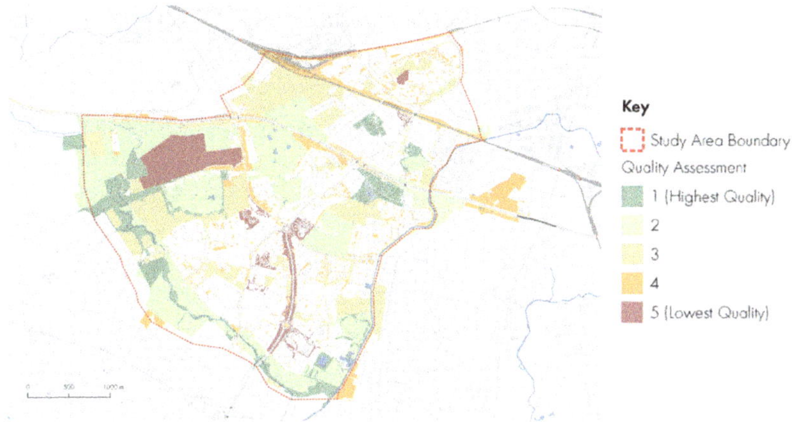

Fig. 3.10 Map showing landscape quality assessment of land around Northolt, 2016.

Source: London Borough of Ealing/Allies and Morrison. *Northolt Framework*. Allies and Morrison, May 2017.

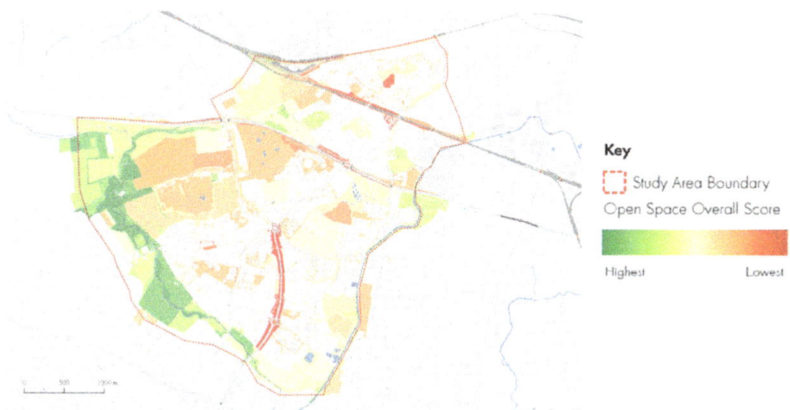

Fig. 3.11 Map showing composite landscape quality assessment around Northolt, 2016.

Source: London Borough of Ealing/Allies and Morrison. *Northolt Framework*. Allies and Morrison, May 2017.

environmental upgrading, for ecological or recreational purposes, might be considered. One of the findings was the difficulty in differentiating between Green Belt and MOL. In planning terms, the degree of protection and the rules applied to any development within the Green Belt and MOL are more or less identical. The study found that there was greater public access to MOL than Green Belt – leading to a conclusion that MOL sits within the city and effectively joins neighbourhoods together, whereas Green Belt specifically separates districts from one another.

The study proceeded to analyse areas that might be released as part of a wider strategy of neighbourhood intensification and densification. This suggested an opportunity for some land exchange, and some release of areas with low amenity value – in particular exhausted gravel extraction sites and disused golf courses. In total some 55 site opportunities were identified representing 160 hectares of land. Not all of these sites would have been suitable for development, but theoretically they could have accommodated up to 13,000 new homes (assuming densities of between 50 and 100 units per hectare).

This detailed study of development opportunities in Northolt concluded that all growth could be accommodated while leaving the Green Belt largely untouched. The approach taken in Northolt was a dynamic study that looked at sophisticated land swaps to rationalise the urban edge. The approach taken in Enfield similarly involved a detailed study of development opportunities, but would not rationalise the urban edge.

Planning and the Green Belt

The English planning system has a high degree of flexibility. When drawing up Statutory Plans different interests are 'balanced' through consultation and negotiation. Individuals and organisations have the rights for representations to be heard by an independent inspectorate. Once a Plan has been approved, each individual development is then decided on its merits with reference to material considerations, the principle one being the Local Plan and national policy guidelines. This is a pragmatic but not necessarily fair process, as it tends in practice to be weighted towards development. In addition, it has been significantly weakened by governments over the past 35 years through cuts in local planning resources. There are few defendable lines in planning, but the Green Belt is one of these. This is not absolute, however, and changes in interpretation of development are made by successive governments. This is undoubtedly leading to the slow erosion of the Green Belt.

In a rational world any assessment of the development potential or otherwise of Green Belt land would be undertaken strategically. Each district differs in character and it would be a reasonable assumption that some areas might be able to accommodate more development than others. This would require comparisons to be made at a regional level. Unfortunately, England currently lacks any organisational capacity to do this. The NPPF is a national planning policy framework, but England is highly unusual in not having a national spatial plan: Wales, Scotland, Northern Ireland and most European countries do. When the 2011 Localism Act abolished the Regional Development Agencies, England was also left without any tier of regional authority. Consequently strategic decisions – whether about airport capacity in the South East or growth corridors related to the new high-speed railway line (HS2) – have no clear forum for debate. Without some form of regional framework, strategic questions on how to meet housing need – whether through new settlement planning, brownfield land development or Green Belt land release – are impossible to resolve. The consequences, as Section 1 on recent Green Belt battles demonstrates, are piecemeal decisions, sub-optimal spatial distribution, a disjuncture between new housing provision, employment and infrastructure, public opposition and political dilemmas.

In the absence of any regional planning mechanism it is up to Local Plans, drawn up by district councils, to make decisions regarding any changes to the Green Belt. This is clearly unsatisfactory for several reasons. The first is strategic. A Local Plan is restricted to a specific local area; it is not able to make wider judgements concerning the appropriateness of development in its own area against any other district. Consequently considerations concerning the future size, shape and direction of growth of cities have no proper forum for consideration, let alone public debate. The absence of a regional planning framework also means that decisions on infrastructure are not related to land use planning.

This is illustrated by many examples including the proposed HS2 railway line, where the siting of stations outside city centres (with a 'park and ride' facility) has no relation to spatial development opportunities at a sub-regional level. The economic policy arguments that should be promoting the regeneration of regional cities in order to rebalance the national economy are generally subordinate to transport criteria. In the case of Green Belt policy, the result is an incremental approach that is likely to be sub-optimal. This is compounded by the imposition of housing targets and their use by planning inspectors on appeal to justify Green Belt loss. The second drawback is political. By devolving decisions on Green Belt release to district councils, it is unlikely that a radical approach to rethinking the Green Belt will ever take place. In such a context so-called NIMBYism is completely understandable. Any councillors brave enough to take on the challenge are unlikely to remain in office for long. The result is a long and unsatisfactory war of attrition that sees the Green Belt slowly eroded (and in the wrong places).

Furthermore, the urban region represents not just opportunities for new housing, but also the chance to generate energy, grow food, clean and store water, recycle and reuse waste materials. Green Belts create/contribute to lower temperatures and mitigate heat waves; they are fundamentally important in building urban resilience. They can also provide a biodiverse ecosystem and a place for recreation, exercise and enjoyment. Any rethinking of Green Belt land therefore also needs to be accompanied by a sophisticated strategy for sustainable development.

Decisions regarding the future of Green Belt land are strategic in nature and should be embedded into regional spatial strategies. For this, regional planning is an essential but missing ingredient. If the debate is centred on the Green Belt then there may also be an argument for Green Belts to be properly planned by a single planning body – or preferably by a regional body that also incorporates metropolitan areas.

Options for capturing land value uplift

Agricultural land in the south-east of England is worth around £20,000 a hectare on average. The same piece of land with a planning consent for residential development on the edge of London is worth £3 to £7 million a hectare.[64] There is an obvious argument to capture this uplift through some form of betterment taxation. The LSE's work cited above explores this concept.[65]

Essentially the proposition is that a percentage of value uplift, considered a windfall, should be taxed. There have been numerous attempts within the planning system to do just this. However, development land taxes of different forms, introduced in 1947, again in 1967 and again in 1976 (with the Development Land Tax), have not been successful. This is largely down to politics. Such legislation has generally been introduced by Labour governments and abolished by Conservative ones. Their introduction has been hampered by the belief that they would be abolished under a change of government. This causes developers to delay their housing projects. The resultant sluggish development market and perceived planning blight is then used to justify scrapping the policy. Although betterment taxes per se have not been used in the UK for over 40 years, stamp duty and planning gain through Community Infrastructure Levy (CIL) or Section 106 agreements are in effect today's quasi-betterment taxes.[66]

An alternative approach would be to introduce specific legislation that allows the state to acquire land at existing use (agricultural) values.

This might relate to a particular area such as the Green Belt or to a particular initiative such as the development of new settlements. The model behind the development of the New Towns in the immediate post-war period was based on the acquisition of land at existing use (agricultural) values. The 1946 New Towns Act incorporated specific powers to buy and sell land, provide infrastructure, utilities and housing. This land was acquired at agricultural values. As already noted in chapter 1, the idea of state intervention to acquire land in response to national needs was well established in the immediate post-war period. The appetite for state intervention diminished in the 1970s onwards and widescale land acquisition was largely abandoned as the UK government moved towards a mixed economy and public/private partnership.

By the end of the 1970s state intervention in direct housing provision and large-scale land purchasing had greatly diminished. As far as the Green Belt was concerned, the Town and Country Planning Act (1947) meant that development could be controlled on open land without resorting to expensive purchase schemes. The Planning Act effectively 'nationalised' development rights in order to plan development properly. In doing this it steered a delicate path between national needs and the jealously guarded rights of the landowner to 'enjoy' their land. Successive governments since have rightly been cautious about intervening in an individual's property rights, and this includes an individual's right to profit from the development of their land. Have circumstances changed that might warrant a new approach? The shift in the role of government from supplier to enabler, especially in the housing sector, that has taken place over the past 35 years has coincided with a significant reduction in house building and growing shortages.

The reduction in state expenditure on housing has been partly offset through placing the burden for the provision of affordable housing and infrastructure on the private sector through Section 106 agreements and Community Infrastructure Levy (CIL) that is effectively a fixed rate development tax. Like betterment levies, planning policy is not a constant. In London, successive Labour and Conservative Mayors have varied the percentage of affordable housing required from developers from less than 35 per cent to 50 per cent, causing considerable uncertainty in the housing development sector. Either way the planning system is increasingly being used to extract public benefits that have traditionally been provided by the state through taxation. Local planning authorities are not in reality the most effective organisations to administer what is in effect taxation. Planners are not trained as accountants. The result is that they are often accused of a lack of transparency and a conflict of interest.

An argument that supports some form of betterment tax or compulsory purchase at existing agricultural values is the fact that it is the grant of consent that conveys the uplift in value, not the development itself. Obtaining a beneficial planning consent involves low costs and limited risk, but it is this that allows the land to be traded as a speculative commodity. The eventual developer who acquires the land pays a high price, takes all of the risks *and* is then taxed through CIL or Section 106. The subsequent squeeze is often manifested in reductions in quality, amenity or in the percentage of affordable housing. Making planning decisions that rely on viability assessments only compounds the situation, as the super profits have already been taken out of the system by the landowner. The introduction of viability assessments has in fact resulted in many substandard schemes that paid too much for the land being approved. Put simply, planning based 'taxes' occur at the wrong stage in the process.

Forms of betterment levy operate in other countries, including Germany. A land readjustment charge, *Umlegung,* is commonly used by public authorities to obtain land for housing development and fund the supporting infrastructure. The consent of landowners is not required; local authorities can take 30 per cent of the value on greenfield land and 10 per cent on brownfield.[67] In addition, the provision of local infrastructure is the responsibility of the local authority which can charge landowners to recover part of its cost. Landowners pay a maximum of 90 per cent when the site is to be developed for the first time and the local authority pays a minimum of 10 per cent.[68]

In 2004 Milton Keynes introduced a Strategic Land and Infrastructure Contract. Effectively a building tariff or roof tax, this was used to fund social and physical infrastructure in the town's strategic expansion areas. Developers agreed to pay standardised contributions of £18,500 per residential dwelling and £260,000 per hectare of commercial land, using Section 106 agreements. Milton Keynes then borrowed money from the Homes and Communities Agency (HCA) to forward-fund infrastructure. This form of prudential borrowing was approved by the Treasury. The charge to the developer was made on completion of the development. The model has not been used elsewhere in the UK, however, although CIL charges are typically around £25,000 per new dwelling in central London.

The research by the Centre for Cities, discussed above, argues for release of land around railway stations and proposes establishing 'Green Belt Development Corporations' (under the powers of the Local Government, Planning and Land Act 1981). The land would be acquired by railway authorities and a development charge of 20 per cent would be made against the uplift in value. Surpluses would be used by local communities for a range of needs including affordable housing. Profits might also be used to reduce public subsidies to the railway companies. Part of the argument is that if some of the uplift in value could be made available to local communities then there would be an incentive for them to release land, which might in turn make development approval easier.[69]

Another proposal to capture value uplift from the planning process was set out by URBED in its winning submission for the 2014 Wolfson Prize for a new Garden City.[70] The submission proposed the extension of an existing, medium-sized settlement to provide housing for an additional 200,000 people. This would be divided into four neighbourhoods of 50,000, each with a secondary school and three primary schools. These were then further divided into smaller neighbourhoods of 10,000 that could support a local centre and employment. The model proposed a form of 'betterment tax' with the land being acquired at near to existing agricultural use value and then being vested in a foundation (a partnership of local authorities, the Local Economic Partnership (LEP) and others, including investors who might only hold a minority stake).

The proposal was based on Dutch and German systems that allow the value generated by development to be invested back into infrastructure. Primary legislation would have been required in the form of a 'Garden Cities Act' to enable this. The foundation body would be both development and management agency. URBED's case for a form of land value capture was based on its conclusion that both physical and social infrastructure should be in place at the beginning of development and therefore requires subsidy. With public finances under pressure, land capture was the obvious solution.

There have been a number of reviews, mainly sponsored by the Labour Party, into responses to the housing crisis. The Lyons Housing Review recommended new powers for local authorities to be able to purchase land compulsorily and the introduction of land taxation.[71] In 2018 the Raynsford Review made a number of significant criticisms of the planning system over the last decade, in particular deregulation and under investment. Its recommendations included:[72]

- Making planning more proactive
- Creating a sub-regional planning framework
- Using stamp duty and capital gains tax from land transactions to fund services for local communities
- That councils should be able to CPO land and take a percentage of the development uplift to fund local planning

Many recent studies such as those by the LSE[73] are now advocating some mechanism to capture a percentage of the increase in land value that occurs when planning consent is granted. In the light of housing pressures and the competing demands for public spending, some form of land value uplift tax would seem to be a solution. The revenues could subsidise affordable housing and fund the purchase of open land for public access and ecological uses. The idea of purchasing large swathes of the Green Belt using public funds would be a return to the original concept of the Green Belt.

Section 3: Conclusions

The creation of the Green Belt was undoubtedly an enlightened approach to urban planning, particularly when set alongside other 20th-century policies that sought to provide decent housing for all, healthy environments and a wide range of civic amenities. These were part of a consensus that was based on a central role for government and the belief that it was possible rationally to plan a better and more equitable future. Public space and the open countryside were seen to be self-evidently part of the public good, even if this good was defined by a relatively small group of professional planners.

The consensus within society that led to the creation of the Green Belt is now under stress. Society has changed and its needs are pluralist. When considering the future of the Green Belt it should be self-evident that an institution designed 70–80 years ago is unlikely to be ideal for today's circumstances. That is not to argue that the Green Belt is outmoded, but its role and purpose, as well as some of its unintended consequences, should be reviewed. The debate concerning Green Belt release is highly emotive, but rarely sophisticated.

As noted above, the wider urban region represents not just opportunities for new housing, but also opportunities to generate energy, grow food, clean and store water, recycle and reuse waste materials. We know that Green Belts can produce or contribute to lower temperatures and mitigate heat waves, with an extremely important role in building urban resilience. They are biodiverse ecosystems and provide places for recreation, exercise and enjoyment. Decisions regarding the future of Green Belt land should therefore be wider than just the provision of housing and must be integrated into regional spatial strategies.

Although Green Belt is not being eroded at an alarming rate, it is being lost, and the rate of loss is increasing. National planning policy has facilitated this through subtle changes in policy guidelines. The imposition of housing targets and the piecemeal responses through local plans is not a rational approach to dealing with such a valuable resource as the countryside surrounding our cities. The incremental loss of Green Belt, driven by development pressures, is fuelling an emotive (and largely unproductive) reaction against new development. Studies show that there is a supply of land within cities that could, in theory, provide new housing without encroaching on Green Belt. The problem is that planning at a local level is not sensitive enough to identify small sites.

Even if it could do so, there are problems in unlocking many of these sites. These sites have often not been developed because there are barriers concerning ownership, access, contamination and viability. Planning restrictions protect other activities such as existing industrial uses and in many cases developing on greenfield sites is seen as an easier option. Other sites, especially out of town shopping, are undoubtedly too valuable in their existing configuration to warrant redevelopment despite the obvious advantages of doing so. The inability to release these sites is an example of the failure of the existing planning system to work proactively. Years of underinvestment in local authorities have made them reactive. In the absence of any mechanism to respond to opportunities within the urban area, pressure mounts on Green Belt sites.

The two case studies of Northolt and Enfield demonstrate that there are other options that might be explored before Green Belt land is built on. The Enfield study does involve loss of strategic industrial land (SIL) that would be contrary to planning policy. But the loss of Green Belt land is also contrary to the intention of planning policy. The Enfield study successfully identifies sites near to good public transport nodes *within the city* as opposed to proposing releasing land around stations in the Green Belt. Moreover, the major land use losses would be to out of town retail that is largely car-based and has undoubtedly contributed to the decline of local town centres. The Northolt study was based on a qualitative assessment of existing open land and proposed a degree of infilling to boost residential densities that in turn would support better local services. The two studies also highlight the fact that planning assessment of vacant and brownfield land is undoubtedly too coarse grained and is constrained by broad assumptions regarding suitability and availability. In the absence of finer grained planning assessments there is almost certainly an underestimate of the amount of land potentially available for development within existing urban areas. As a consequence there are dual pressures both to release Green Belt *and* to build at very high densities on the brownfield land.

The missing element in all of the arguments for and against release of Green Belt land is a discussion of the role of planning. In England there is no system for making strategic decisions on a regional basis. An *effective* planning system would be able to assess land availability and demand on a regional basis. It would then develop long-term spatial plans that would consider the shape and distribution of new development and relate this to the necessary transport and infrastructure investment. The timeframe would need to be at least 25 years and reviews should be conducted on no less than a 15-year cycle. Such a system would need to be proactive and to have the powers and resources to intervene in the market at scale.

Possible models would be variations on the Regional Development Agencies (abolished in 2011 and requiring new legislation) or Development Corporations that could be set up under existing powers. In other words, the Green Belt should be subject to a coherent planning regime.

The second issue is around land value capture. By the time most land enters the planning process values have already been inflated and any financial flexibility has been removed from the system. The result is a struggle for the planning system to extract value from schemes that already have extremely tight parameters. This results in delays and cost reductions that mitigate against design quality and high environmental performance. As a consequence, housing prices remain high. A reliance solely on the market through easing Green Belt restrictions is likely to make brownfield development less attractive. It is also unlikely to deliver affordable housing to areas where it is most needed.

A possible response could be to set up regional planning agencies based on city regions with the powers of Development Corporations. This would require primary legislation, but the Green Belt is already specifically designated. A Green Belt Development Corporation could have the primary purpose to *protect and enhance* the Green Belt (and even to look for possible extensions). It would plan strategically and consider release on a set of clear criteria. If it had powers to acquire land at agricultural values and capture the uplift, this Corporation would have funds to acquire further land for permanent open access or ecological enhancement, including rewilding, and for energy generation and flood mitigation. Land profits would also cross-subsidise both new physical and social infrastructure and affordable housing in areas where it is needed. Finally, a planned approach to the Green Belt would enable environmental and resilience planning to take place on a regional level. The scope for the city and its hinterlands to mitigate climate change is developed further in chapter 4.

There are overwhelming arguments for the reassessment of the Green Belt to accommodate growth and respond to climate change through the planned management of the urban hinterland. But any reappraisal should be strategic, planned and based on a thorough understanding of the varying qualities and potentials of each and every part of the Green Belt. The crux of the debate is whether the presently designated Green Belt area still fulfils its original objectives, whether there are trade-offs at the margin for the Green Belt land to deliver present policy requirements and others such as housing or whether circumstances have changed and a new approach is needed, particularly to mitigate climate change. The alternative is piecemeal erosion through development that is divorced from any rational planning context. If a fundamental reappraisal is beyond the present capabilities of government and the planning system, then there is a compelling argument for the Green Belt to be left untouched for future generations. Once lost, it will be lost forever.

Notes

1. MHCLG 2019.
2. Office for National Statistics 2019.
3. Barker 2004.
4. NAO 2019.
5. Booth 2019.
6. GLA 2018.
7. GLA 2014.
8. Lyons Housing Review 2014.
9. Barker 2014.
10. SMF 2007.
11. NFB 2019.
12. Papworth 2015.
13. Malnick 2018a; Clarke 2018.
14. Bahar 2019.
15. Malnick 2018b.
16. Wright 2019.
17. Centre for Policy Studies 2018.
18. London First 2019.
19. The arguments against HS2, for example, are focusing on the loss of ancient woodlands and wildlife habitat (rather than the potential negative impact on local house prices).
20. Priestley 1934.
21. DCLG 2008/9, 2009–10, 2010–11, 2011–12, 2012–13.
22. MHCLG 2019.
23. CPRE 2018.
24. Maidment 2018.
25. The London Green Belt Council brings together over 100 organisations including councils, residents and environmental groups with a shared concern for London's Green Belt. https://londongreenbeltcouncil.org.uk/.
26. LGBC 2019.
27. HM Government 2018.

28. LGBC 2019, p.12
29. LGBC 2019, pp. 5–6.
30. Barker Review 2006.
31. Cheshire and Carozzi 2019.
32. Cheshire and Carozzi 2019.
33. Foresight 2010.
34. Scott 2017.
35. Centre for Policy Studies 2018.
36. Wiles 2014.
37. Hammond 2012.
38. Save Stourbridge Green Belt 2019.
39. Smith 2019.
40. Change.org 2019.
41. Edgar 2018.
42. Popplewell 2019.
43. CPRE Essex 2019.
44. Turley Associates 2014.
45. Miner 2017.
46. The New Homes Bonus is a grant paid by central government to local councils to reflect and incentivise housing growth in their areas. www.parliament.uk 2017.
47. Brentwood Borough Council 2018b.
48. London Green Belt Council 2019.
49. Live tables on land use change statistics. Ministry of Housing, Communities and Local Government, May 2018.
50. Bishop and Timmerman 2019.
51. CPRE 2010.
52. Brentwood Borough Council 2018a.
53. Shoard 2002.
54. Scalbert 2015.
55. HTA Design 2015.
56. Mace et al. 2016.
57. Mace et al. 2018.
58. Cheshire and Buyuklieva 2019.
59. Edgar 2016.
60. London First 2015.
61. Wright 2018.
62. Enfield Society 2019.
63. Northolt Study: Allies and Morrison/London Borough of Ealing 2017.
64. MHCLG 2017.
65. Cheshire and Buyuklieva 2019.
66. McAllister 2019.
67. Zaborowski 2018.
68. German Federal Building Code (Section 129).
69. Cheshire and Buyuklieva 2019.
70. URBED 2014.
71. Lyons Housing Review 2014.
72. TCPA 2018.
73. Cheshire and Buyuklieva 2019.

References

Allies and Morrison/London Borough of Ealing. *Northolt Framework*. Allies and Morrison, May 2017.

Bahar, U. 'How to Get Planning Permission for Building on the Green Belt in the UK', *Urbanist Architecture* (2019). https://urbanistarchitecture.co.uk/how-to-get-planning-permission-for-building-on-greenbelt-land-in-the-uk/.

Barker, K. 'Report of Housing Supply: Final report and recommendations'. London: HMSO, 2004.

Barker, K. 'Review of Land Use Planning'. London: HMSO, December 2006.

Barker, K. *Housing: Where's the Plan?* London: London Publishing Partnership, 2014.

Bishop, P. and Timmerman, R. 'Housing Sprint: Increasing housing supply and affordability', October 2019. https://www.sbs.ox.ac.uk/sites/default/files/2019-09/Housing_sprint_final_report.pdf.

Booth, Robert. 'Half of Councils Expected to Miss Housebuilding Targets', *The Guardian*, 8 February 2019. https://www.theguardian.com/society/2019/feb/08/half-councils-expected-miss-housebuilding-targets-england. Accessed 11 November 2019.

Brentwood Borough Council. 'Brentwood Green Belt Study: Overview and technical note'. Brentwood Borough Council, 5 February 2018a. http://www.brentwood.gov.uk/pdf/06022018152429000000.pdf . Accessed 11 December 2019.

Brentwood Borough Council. 'Green Belt Study Part I: London Metropolitan Green Belt overview' (Report Reference: CE-BW-0585-RP06 - FINAL 01 November 2018b). https://www.brentwood.gov.uk/pdf/06112018150226000000.pdf. Accessed 12 December 2019.

Campaign to Protect Rural England (CPRE). 'Green Belts: A greener future', 27 January 2010. https://www.cpre.org.uk/resources/green-belts-a-greener-future/. Accessed 4 January 2020.

Campaign to Protect Rural England (CPRE). 'State of the Green Belt 2018', August 2018. https://www.cpre.org.uk/resources/housing-and-planning/green-belts/item/4931-state-of-the-green-belt-2018. Accessed 12 December 2019.

Campaign to Protect Rural England (CPRE). 'Space to Breathe', October 2019. https://www.cpre.org.uk/resources/housing-and-planning/green-belts/item/5189-space-to-breathe?highlight=WyJzcGFjZSIsIidzcGFjZSIsInNwYWNlJyIsInNwYWNlJywiLCInc3>. Accessed 11 November 2019.

Campaign to Protect Rural England (CPRE) Essex. 'Elections Prove our Countryside Matters to People, says Green Belt Council', 17 June 2019. http://cpressex.org.uk/elections-prove-our-countryside-matters-to-people-says-green-belt-council/.

Centre for Policy Studies, 'Housing Poll September 2018', 7 October 2018. https://www.comresglobal.com/polls/centre-for-policy-studies-housing-poll-september-2018/. Accessed 28 October 2018.

Change.org. 'Enfield's Green Belt and Open Spaces Under Threat'. 2019. https://www.change.org/p/enfield-local-authority-protect-the-green-belt-and-open-spaces-in-enfield. Accessed 6 January 2020.

Cheshire, P. and Buyuklieva, B. 'Homes on the Right Tracks: Greening the Green Belt to solve the housing crisis'. London: LSE Centre for Cities, September 2019. http://eprints.lse.ac.uk/102337/1/Cheshire_homes_on_the_right_tracks_published.pdf. Accessed 12 February 2020.

Cheshire, P. and Carozzi, F. 'Housing Sprint: Land Report', Table 3. London: LSE, 2019. http://eprints.lse.ac.uk/102339/3/Cheshire_housing_sprint_land_report_published.pdf. Accessed 14 February 2020.

Clarke, S. 'Allowing Building Within Half a Mile of Train Stations Would Free Up Enough Land for 1.5m New Homes', *Daily Telegraph*, 8 September 2018. https://www.telegraph.co.uk/news/2018/09/08/allowing-building-within-half-mile-train-stations-would-free/. Accessed 28 November 2019.

Department of Communities and Local Government (DCLG). *Local Planning Authority Green Belt Statistics: England 2008/9*. Planning: Statistical Release, 16 October 2014. London: HMSO.

Department of Communities and Local Government (DCLG). *Local Planning Authority Green Belt Statistics: England (2008/9, 2009–2010, 2010–2011, 2011–2012, 2012–2013)*. Planning: Statistical Releases. https://webarchive.nationalarchives.gov.uk/20120919203331/; http://www.communities.gov.uk/documents/statistics/pdf/1210399.pdf.

Design for London. *Green Infrastructure and Open Environment: The all London green grid*. London Plan Supplementary Guidance. London: GLA, 7 June 2011.

Edgar, L. 'Replace London's Green Belt with "Green Web" to Deliver Housing', *The Planner*, 21 October 2016. https://www.theplanner.co.uk/news/replace-london%E2%80%99s-green-belt-with-%E2%80%%2098green-web%E2%80%99-to-deliver-housing. Accessed 12 November 2019.

Edgar, L. 'Brokenshire Prevents Adoption of East Hertfordshire's Local Plan', *The Planner*, 12 September 2018. https://www.theplanner.co.uk/news/brokenshire-prevents-adoption-of-east-hertfordshire%E2%80%99s-local-plan. Accessed 12 November 2019.

Enfield Society. *Space to Build in Enfield*. London: The Enfield Society with Enfield RoadWatch and the CPRE, January 2019. http://www.cprelondon.org.uk/projects/item/2427-space-to-build-in-enfield. Accessed 15 November 2019.

Foresight. 'Land Use Futures: Making the most of land in the 21st century'. Foresight Final Project Report. London: Government Office for Science, 2010. https://assets.publishing.service.gov.uk/government/uploads/system/uploads/attachment_data/file/288843/10-631-land-use-futures.pdf.

German Federal Building Code (Section 129). https://germanlawarchive.iuscomp.org/?p=649.

Greater London Authority (GLA). *London Strategic Housing Market Assessment*. London: GLA, January 2014. https://www.london.gov.uk/file/15571/download?token=q4aeX4gP. Accessed 16 September 2019.

Greater London Authority (GLA). *London Plan*, 2016. London: GLA, January 2017. https://www.london.gov.uk/what-we-do/planning/london-plan/current-london-plan/london-plan-2016-pdf. Accessed 25 September 2019.

Greater London Authority (GLA). *London Housing Strategy 2018*. London: GLA, May 2018. https://www.london.gov.uk/sites/default/files/2018_lhs_london_housing_strategy.pdf. Accessed 25 September 2019.

Hammond, Ed. 'St Albans Resists Greenbelt Development', *Financial Times*, 7 September 2012. https://www.ft.com/content/b24be9da-f8f7-11e1-b4ba-00144feabdc0. Accessed 21 December 2019.

HM Government. *A Green Future: Our 25 Year Plan to Improve the Environment*. London: HMSO, 2018. https://assets.publishing.service.gov.uk/government/uploads/system/uploads/attachment_data/file/693158/25-year-environment-plan.pdf.

HTA Design, Pollard Thomas Edwards, Savills and Nathaniel Lichfield and Partners. *Transforming Suburbia: Supurbia Semi-Permissive*, 2015. https://www.pollardthomasedwards.co.uk/download/supurbia-semipermissive_v5_LR.pdf. Accessed 16 January 2020.

KentOnline. https://www.kentonline.co.uk/tunbridge-wells/news/council-told-this-is-madness-210656/. Accessed 20 November 2019.

London First. 'The Green Belt: A Place for Londoners?', February 2015. https://www.londonfirst.co.uk/sites/default/files/documents/2018-05/Green-Belt.pdf. Accessed 4 December 2019.

London First. 'Time for Government to Review Outdated Green Belt Rules', 18 September 2019. https://www.londonfirst.co.uk/news-publications/news/time-for-government-to-review-outdated-green-belt-rules-london-first. Accessed 4 December 2019.

London Green Belt Council. 'Safe Under Us? – Two Years On', January 2019. http://londongreenbeltcouncil.org.uk/wp-content/uploads/2019/01/Further-serious-loss-of-LGB.pdf.

Lyons Housing Review, Labour Party, October 2014. https://www.yourbritain.org.uk/uploads/editor/files/The_Lyons_Housing_Review_2.pdf. Accessed 4 December 2019.

McAllister, P. 'The taxing problems of land value capture, planning obligations and viability tests: some reasonable models?', *Town Planning Review* 90 (4) (2019): 429–51. https://www.ucl.ac.uk/bartlett/construction/sites/bartlett/files/the_=taxing_=problems_=of_=land_=value_=mcallister_=april_=2019.pdf. Accessed 15 October 2019.

Mace, A., Blanc, F., Gordon, I. and Scanlon, K. *A 21st Century Metropolitan Green Belt*. London: LSE, 2016. http://eprints.lse.ac.uk/id/eprint/68012.

Mace, A., Blanc, F. and Mossa, A. 'The London Cambridge Corridor – Making More of Green Belt', LSE with Levitt-Bernstein, February 2018. https://www.levittbernstein.co.uk/site/assets/files/3039/london-cambridge_corridor_report.pdf. Accessed 6 February 2020.

Maidment, Jack. 'England's Green Belt Suffers Biggest Reduction in Eight Years as Councils Remove Protections to Build Houses', *Daily Telegraph*, 4 October 2018. https://www.telegraph.co.uk/politics/2018/10/04/englands-green-belt-suffers-biggest-reduction-eight-years-councils/. Accessed 10 November 2019.

Malnick, Edward. 'Theresa May Urged to Drop Personal Allegiances and Allow New Homes on Greenbelt Land to Help Solve Housing Crisis', 2018a. https://www.telegraph.co.uk/news/2018/09/08/theresa-may-urged-drop-personal-allegiances-allow-new-homes/. Accessed 23 November 2019.

Malnick, Edward. 'Cabinet Urges May to Build on Green Belt', *Daily Telegraph*, 6 October 2018b. https://www.telegraph.co.uk/news/2018/10/06/cabinet-urges-may-build-green-belt/. Accessed 10 November 2019.

Miner, Paul. 'Green Belt: When exceptional circumstances aren't exceptional', 2017. Campaign to Protect Rural England (CPRE). https://www.cpre.org.uk/magazine/opinion/item/4552-housing-white-paper-empty-promises-on-green-belt. Accessed 3 November 2019.

Ministry of Housing, Communities and Local Government (MHCLG). 'Land Value Estimates for Policy Appraisal 2017'. https://www.gov.uk/government/publications/land-value-estimates-for-policy-appraisal-2017. Accessed 4 November 2019.

Ministry of Housing, Communities and Local Government (MHCLG). *Local Planning Authority Green Belt: England 2018/19*. Planning: Statistical Release, 18 October 2019. https://assets.publishing.service.gov.uk/government/uploads/system/uploads/attachment_=data/file/856100/Green_=Belt_=Statistics_=England_=2018-19.pdf. Accessed 4 November 2019.

National Audit Office (NAO). *Planning for New Homes*, 8 February 2019. https://www.nao.org.uk/wp-content/uploads/2019/02/Planning-for-new-homes.pdf. Accessed 5 November 2019.

National Federation of Builders (NFB). *Reimagining the Greenbelt is Vital to Preserving It*, 13 May 2019. https://www.politicshome.com/news/uk/economy/construction-industry/press-release/national-federation-builders/103823/reimagining.

Office for National Statistics. *Housing Affordability in England and Wales: 2018*, 28 March 2019. https://www.ons.gov.uk/peoplepopulationandcommunity/housing/bulletins/housingaffordabilityinenglandandwales/2018. Accessed 12 February 2020.

Papworth T. *The Green Noose*. The Adam Smith Institute, January 2015. https://www.adamsmith.org/research/the-green-noose. Accessed 3 December 2019.

Popplewell, Erica. 'To What Extent is the Environment Shaping National Politics?', *LocalGov*, 15 May 2019. https://www.localgov.co.uk/To-what-extent-is-the-environment-shaping-national-politics/47413. Accessed 15 January 2020.

Priestley, J.B. *English Journey*. London: Victor Gollancz, 1934.

Save Stourbridge Green Belt, 2019. https://www.stourbridgegreenbelt.co.uk/. Accessed 12 December 2019.

Scalbert, Irénée. 'London After the Green Belt', *AA Files* no. 66, 2015. https://www.thomasdanegallery.com/usr/documents/press/download_=url/510/ml-aa-files-2013.pdf. Accessed 14 September 2019.

Scott, Alister. '*Should Britain Build on its Green Spaces to Solve its Housing Crisis?*', *Independent*, February 2017. https://www.independent.co.uk/environment/should-britain-build-on-its-green-spaces-to-solve-the-housing-crisis-a7568341.html. Accessed 5 January 2020.

Shoard, Marion. 'Edgelands'. In *Remaking the Landscape*, edited by Jennifer Jenkins, 117–46. London: Profile Books, 2002.

Social Market Foundation (SMF). *Should the Green Belt Be Preserved*? Social Market Foundation Internal Commission, August 2007. http://www.smf.co.uk/wp-content/uploads/2007/08/Publication-Should-the-Green-Belt-be-preserved.pdf. Accessed 11 November 2019.

Smith, A. 'Tunbridge Wells Council Under Fire Over Local Plan Proposals', *KentOnline*, 17 August 2019. https://www.kentonline.co.uk/tunbridge-wells/news/council-told-this-is-madness-210656/.

Town and Country Planning Association (TCPA). *Planning 2020: Final report of the Raynsford Review of Planning in England*, 2018. https://www.tcpa.org.uk/Handlers/Download.ashx?IDMF=30864427-d8dc-4b0b-88ed-c6e0f08c0edd. Accessed 4 June 2019.

Turley Associates. 'Neighbourhood Planning: Plan and Deliver?' March 2014. Quoted in Derounian, J. 'It's Neighbourhood Planning, Jim… But Not As We Know It', *Town and Country Planning* 85 (3) (2016): 142–4.

URBED. *Uxcester: Garden City*. Final Report: Wolfson Economics Prize 2014. http://urbed.coop/sites/default/files/20140815%20URBED%20Wolfson%20Stage%202_=low%20res3.pdf.

Wiles, Colin. 'Why the Nimbys are Winning the UK's Housing Battles', *The Guardian*, 22 April 2014. https://www.theguardian.com/housing-network/2014/apr/22/nimbys-winning-housing-battles. Accessed 23 November 2019.

Williams-Ellis, Clough. *England and the Octopus*. London: Geoffrey Bless, 1928.

Wright, Charles. 'Enfield: Council's Green Belt Building Plans Face More Than One Shade of Political Resistance', *OnLondon*, 12 December 2018. https://www.onlondon.co.uk/enfield-councils-green-belt-building-plans-face-more-than-one-shade-of-political-resistance/. Accessed 18 November 2019.

Wright, O. 'We Must Build Homes on the Green Belt, Insists Rees-Mogg', *The Times*, 22 July 2019. https://www.thetimes.co.uk/article/we-must-build-homes-on-the-green-belt-insists-rees-mogg-7sk2qbnjm. Accessed 23 February 2020.

www.parliament.uk. 'The New Homes Bonus Scheme (England)', 24 July 2017. https://researchbriefings.parliament.uk/ResearchBriefing/Summary/SN05724.

Zaborowski, Tomasz. 'Land Acquisition and Land Value Capture Instruments as Determinants of Public Urban Infrastructure Provision: A comparison of the Polish legal framework with its German counterpart', *Geographia Polonica* 91 (3) (2018): 353–69. http://rcin.org.pl/Content/66344/WA51_=86058_=r2018-t91-no3_=G-Polonica-Zaborowsk.pdf.

Chapter 4
The 'Beltscape': new horizons for the city in its natural region

Rob Roggema

Introduction

This chapter considers the relationship between the city and its hinterland with particular reference to the Netherlands. The concept of the Green Belt is taken as the starting point of reference for Dutch regional and national planning approaches. The Randstad, Holland's Green Heart, and the policy to keep cities small and separated by open spaces have been consistent since the 1950s, but it appears that this concept is being eroded under current urban pressures. New concepts are now required if ecology and the landscape are to keep their quality. The 'Beltscape' is proposed as a promising concept in which not only the landscape is protected, but there is also space for useful functions such as growing food, generating renewable energy, increasing biodiversity and purifying water. Finally, the 'Beltscape' can provide the urban population with a clean and healthy environment.

Green spaces in and around the city are under constant and permanent pressure. They face either further urbanisation or a decline into neglected, in-between landscapes that are partly, but not really, urban. Cities and governments seek the preservation of these seemingly green areas, but often ignore the key considerations of their function. It is only on the regional map they appear to be green. The core question in this chapter is whether these areas, the former Green Belts, should be allowed to evolve as dymanic new urban centres or whether the notion of open green landscapes should be permanently retained.

What is actually protected by trying to consolidate these areas as they are? In general the quality and amenity of the housing in these areas is often poor, agricultural production is low and the ecological quality is evenly substandard. In reality, some of these areas are currently dominated by waste incinerators, camp sites, car cemeteries, sewage plants and other marginal uses. The Green Belt might be an historic relic, but it is still highly valued, at least in the minds of urban planners and landscape architects, and this makes debates about its future contentious.

However, this 'relic' is now up for re-evaluation. Growing (and often uncoordinated) pressures from urban growth are unlikely to add to the spatial quality, functionality or future-proofing of the urban landscape. Because the space on the urban fringe is underutilised, it is often seen as a potential opportunity for development and alternative uses. In order to fulfil its original role as a buffer between settlements and a reserve of agricultural and recreational spaces, the Green Belt area needs to undergo spatial and functional reappraisal. New demands are emerging to provide resources in or near the city – for example regenerative ecologies, food, water and energy generation. Contemporary social visions and constructs need to be accommodated, leading to a new relationship between city and landscape. Urbanisation and land use need to be reconsidered. New urban landscape concepts, as well as new demands and new thinking around the densities and concentration of urban areas, are leading to a new philosophy in favour of green spaces in the urban fringe.

In this chapter the current state of Green Belts is analysed, after which the intrinsic concept, adapted internationally and improved in innovative spatial concepts, is discussed. The next questions posed are how could the Green Belt concept be rejuvenated and what might this mean for the spatial configuration of urban landscapes? Later in the chapter new demands and uses to shape these landscapes are brought to the fore, and the ways in which these are used to form a new vision for a future 'Beltscape' explored. The chapter ends with some conclusions and further recommendations.

Green Belts in context

As discussed elsewhere in this book, Green Belts in their modern form originated in the London agglomeration over a century ago. Developed in response to the rapid urbanisation of the 19th century, the concept of both limiting urban growth and protecting open countryside was adopted as a planning strategy. From a landscape in which urban concentrations appeared as small towns, the urban landscape transformed itself into an urban agglomeration with green concentrations in it: an 'urban inversion landscape'.[1] Through defining urban form by its spatial boundaries, planning became a discipline of limitation. Instead of determining the road system, then land use, then landscape, the policy moved towards determining the landscape first, then considering land uses and finally the supporting road systems. Haagse Beemden, a precinct within the city of Breda applied the latter principle consciously in the 1970s – since when it has been a leading way of thinking on which to base the relationship between the urban and the landscape.

In the Netherlands the permanent protection of open land without clearly determined programmes for use led, over time, to many of these areas within the urban agglomeration becoming transformed into urban fringes; their land uses could not find a place anywhere else. These areas lost their intrinsic ecological and recreational values and many became car cemeteries, camp sites and logistical centres. These warehouse boxes and glasshouses, ever increasing in size, dominate the landscape at an increasing, uncontrolled rate.[2] More recently sewage plants, wind parks, recycling stations and many other uses have been added, creating a peri-urban landscape that is only preserved through a sense of nostalgia.

In London, at a very early stage of the urbanisation process, urban sprawl was limited by introducing the Green Belt.[3] The Abercrombie Plan (1944) enclosed an urban conurbation with a radius of 45 km, surrounded by an *external* belt of open green space that was to be kept free of future urban growth. Similarly, in the Netherlands, the Randstad – consisting of the larger cities of Amsterdam, Rotterdam, The Hague and Utrecht – was limited in its growth through the configuration of the 'Green Heart'. Since 1956 this *internal* green space of 40 by 50 km has been supposed to be kept free of major urban development.[4] In both examples, planners sought to restrict urban development through the permanent preservation of green open space.

Currently, however, large parts of Green Belts appear as lost spaces – indifferent, undervalued, in-between areas that are urbanising at an increasing rate. As such their potential role in regional spatial development is underestimated and poorly understood. They could play a crucial future role in supporting human wellbeing and improving degraded ecosystems, but to do so they require a radical reinvention of existing spatial approaches.

Importing ideas for the Green Belt

Since its emergence, the Green Belt concept has been exported from the UK to many countries and has been adapted to local circumstances. In this process many other countries have learned from the spatial features that Green Belts offer and have implemented green spaces within a range of their own conurbations. This process of adaptation between different countries is covered in chapter 2. In the Netherlands, for example, the concept has been used explicitly (more implicitly in the national policy) in the designation of buffer zones to separate cities, in constituting the 'Green Heart' of Holland, in the design of national strategies such as the Ecological Main Structure[5] and in developing strategies for separating green and urban land uses.

Fig. 4.1 Map showing buffer zones in the Netherlands, 2011.

Source: CBS, PBL, RIVM, WUR. *Ontwikkelingen in Rijksbufferzones, 2000–2017* (indicator 2010, versie 07, 6 September 2018). www.lo.nl. Centraal Bureau voor de Statistiek (CBS), Den Haag; Planbureau voor de Leefomgeving (PBL), Den Haag; Rijksinstituut voor Volksgezondheid en Milieu (RIVM), Bilthoven; and Wageningen University and Research WUR, Wageningen, 2018.

Buffer zones: separating the city from the land

In the late 1950s the Dutch National Government first adopted the buffer zone policy in its First National Plan, especially in Randstad Holland.[6] The initial goal of these zones was to safeguard the open and unbuilt space in between urban districts and to keep these separated. From the beginning, the policy aimed at using planning instruments to achieve this. These zones not only separated urban areas, but also incorporated other land use such as forestry, ecology and leisure. They also protected landscape, an important feature in these areas, through regulation in spatial land use plans at both regional and local levels. The 'Werkcommissie Westen des Lands' (Working Committee for the Western Netherlands) formulated the policy that has determined Dutch western landscape ever since and inspired the origin of the Randstad and Green Heart concept:

> When developments are left to autonomous drivers, the main advantages of a Dutch Randstad in comparison with foreign conurbations will be lost: its spatial distinct cities of a moderate size. Therefore, it will be necessary to construct a separative zone of about four kilometers in between cities.[7]

The policy was based upon three main lines of thought:

1. To preserve the historical nodes on the urban ring as permanent but spatially separated gravity centres
2. To preserve the agricultural centre as a core space of large size
3. To allow outward expansion of the entire Randstad

The principle of easy access to the countryside ultimately limits the size of agglomerations. Indirectly this implies letting smaller core settlements grow and allows the development of new towns. The accompanying map (Fig. 4.2) illustrates these objectives. In doing so it reveals the tension between urban developments and the desire to keep spaces green and open in the centre (the Green Heart) and in between urban elements. Initially these zones were to be kept open purely through the use of planning instruments. However, in 1964 financial budgets were reserved in the national budget to purchase strategically located land in the buffer zones.

In subsequent national planning documents, the buffer zone policy was constantly reaffirmed. It was incorporated in the First National Plan on Spatial Policy[8] and consolidated in the Urbanisation Policy

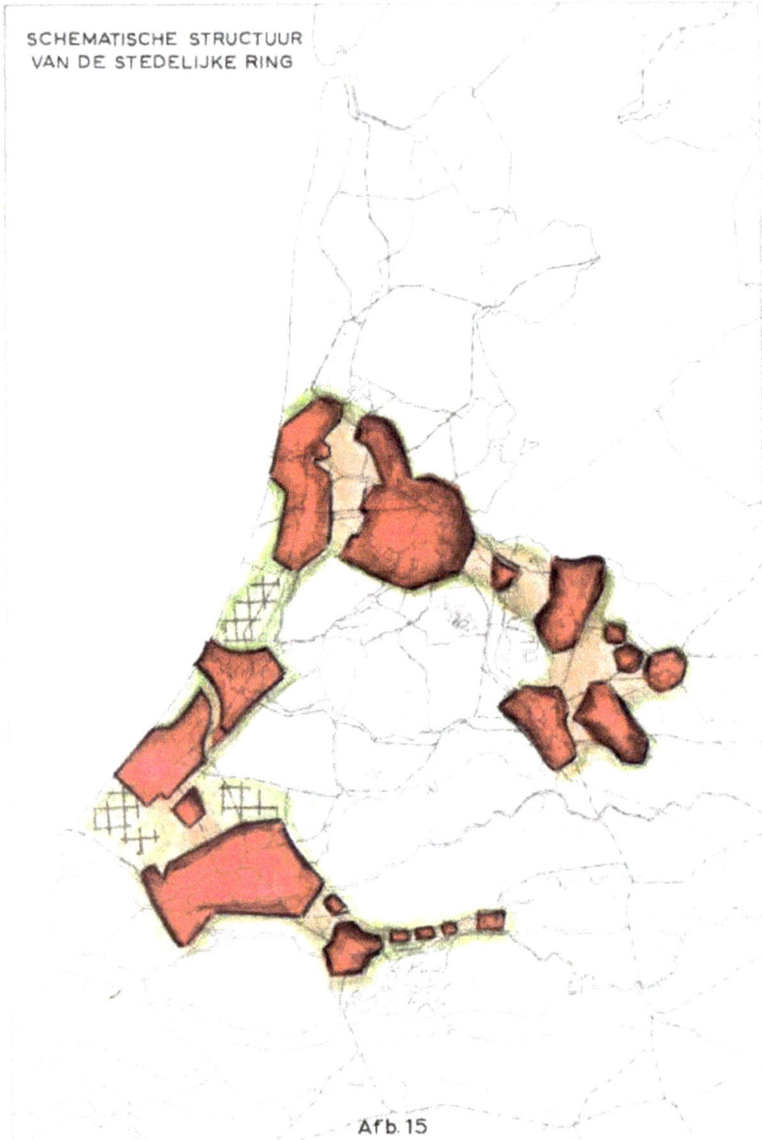

Fig. 4.2 Map showing the schematic structure of the urban ring, including Randstad, the buffer zones and the Green Heart, 1958.

Source: Werkcommissie Westen des Lands (Working Committee for the Western Netherlands). *De ontwikkeling van het westen des lands*, deel 1 rapport. Den Haag: Rijksdienst voor het Nationale Plan, 1958.

in 1977.[9] In this spatial policy document functions such as recreation, nature and agriculture were seen as the main means to implement the objectives for the buffer zones. In 1988, in the Fourth National Plan on Spatial Policy, this concept was further developed and detailed.[10] In the Fourth Plan-Extra (a new national plan formally seen as a modified version of the Fourth, but with its own status),[11] the buffer zones were transformed from planning zones that restricted development into areas that create an added value for recreation, nature and landscape. In 1995 the buffer zones in the Randstad area were formally taken up in the Randstadgroenstructuur.[12]

The implementation of the buffer zone projects is embedded in land consolidation projects (*Landinrichtingsprojecten*) and in Strategic Green projects. Two-thirds of the cost of acquiring land for these projects was financed through the budget of the Ministry of Spatial Planning (VROM); the remaining one-third of the cost came from the Ministry of Agriculture (LNV) and is secured in Buffer Zone Covenants.[13]

In the Fifth National Spatial Plan (1999–2018), the special policy for these buffer zones was dismantled and replaced by a series of regional parks.[14] Analysis shows that these buffer zones have been successful in maintaining the separation of cities and are still substantially less urbanised than the areas outside these zones.[15]

The 'Green Heart': an inside Green Belt

When the founding fathers of Dutch national planning assembled in the Commission for the Western Netherlands (1950–8), they conceived the 'Green Heart' as the essential component of the Randstad (Fig. 4.3).[16] There is an underlying metaphor in this policy – that of the country as a body, whose wellbeing is vitally dependent on the health of its heart. Together Randstad and the Green Heart are at the core of what is termed Dutch 'planning doctrine',[17] with the Green Heart being incorporated into policy for the first time around 1960.[18] In the first National Plan on Spatial Planning,[19] the Green Heart was formally recognised as a spatial policy, based on the work of the 'Werkcommissie Westen des Lands' (Working Committee for the Western Netherlands) (see above). In this the cities, separated by buffer zones, form a ring of urbanisation around a green and open countryside – a policy that enables cities to keep their own identity, size and scale. Up to this point there had been relatively little public appreciation for this internal open area of man-made landscape, but it was soon to become the icon of Dutch planning.[20]

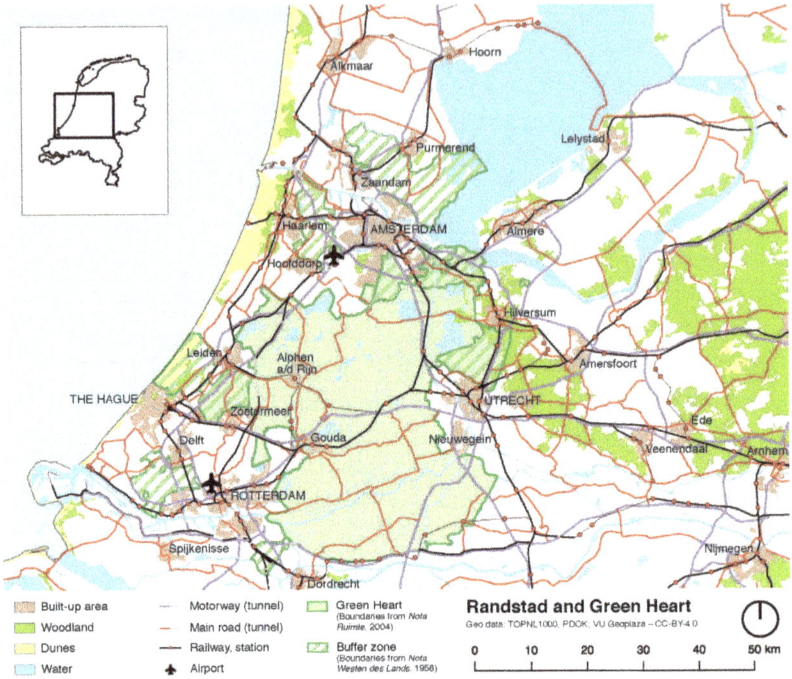

Fig. 4.3 Map showing the Green Heart inside the Randstad Holland, 2008.

Source: Koomen et al. 'Open-Space Preservation in the Netherlands: Planning, practice and prospects', *Land Use Policy* 25 (3) (2008): 361–77.

Currently the Green Heart is still a large open area in the centre of the Randstad Holland. It is a highly diverse region as far as landscape and land use are concerned (Table 4.1) and it derives its identity from the fact that it is surrounded by a girdle of urban areas: the Randstad Ring. This consists of four large city regions (Amsterdam, The Hague, Rotterdam and Utrecht) and six smaller ones (Haarlem, Leiden, Dordrecht, Amersfoort, Hilversum and Almere). These cities combine with the Green Heart to form a complete whole.[21]

The Green Heart covers an area of about 1600 km^2; its purpose is defined as preventing the individual cities from converging into a single urbanised area. Within the Green Heart are 70 local municipalities, 43 of which fall completely within its boundaries. The Green Heart landscape consists to a large extent of agricultural land, mainly used as pasture. Between 1996 and 2006, however, the region has witnessed changes in

Table 4.1 Land use in the Green Heart, 2012

LU/LC class	Total area (2006) in hectares
Transport	5,184
Built-up	9,499
Others	3,553
Open spaces	1,604
Recreation	4,177
Agriculture	122,688
Nature	5,048
Water bodies	15,585

Source: Fazal et al. 'Interpretation of Trends in Land Transformations – A case of Green Heart region (The Netherlands)', *Natural Resources* 3 (2012): 107–17.

land use (Table 4.1). Agricultural land is the only category losing area – a total of 3,650 hectares (a decrease of 28.9 per cent) has been lost. Of this, roughly 1,500 hectares were transformed into built-up areas and transport infrastructure, with another 1,500 hectares changing to open space for nature conservation and recreation.[22] Over time the Green Heart and Randstad have evolved into a polycentric delta-metropolis.[23]

The policies described in the National Plans were incorporated in Structure Schemes (at national level) and Structure Plans (at regional/provincial level). These planning instruments direct the spatial policies and planning at municipal level, which in turn require approval from the higher tiers of government. The task of identifying green open spaces has now been decentralised to municipalities following a new law in 2008. At first local municipalities were given the simple quantitative task of safeguarding green space within a certain time period, but they were later given the task of developing their own policies and plans. Under the new Spatial Planning Law, the responsibility for spatial policies remains at the local level;[24] higher levels of government may only intervene when a national or regional interest is challenged. These interests are set out in the national legislation described above.

The 'Ecologische Hoofdstructuur' (EHS): an ecological structure plan for the Netherlands

In 1990 the Dutch government started a nationwide project of developing a network of nature priority areas.[25] This network is called the *Ecologische*

Table 4.2 Changes of land use in the buffer zones, 2000–17

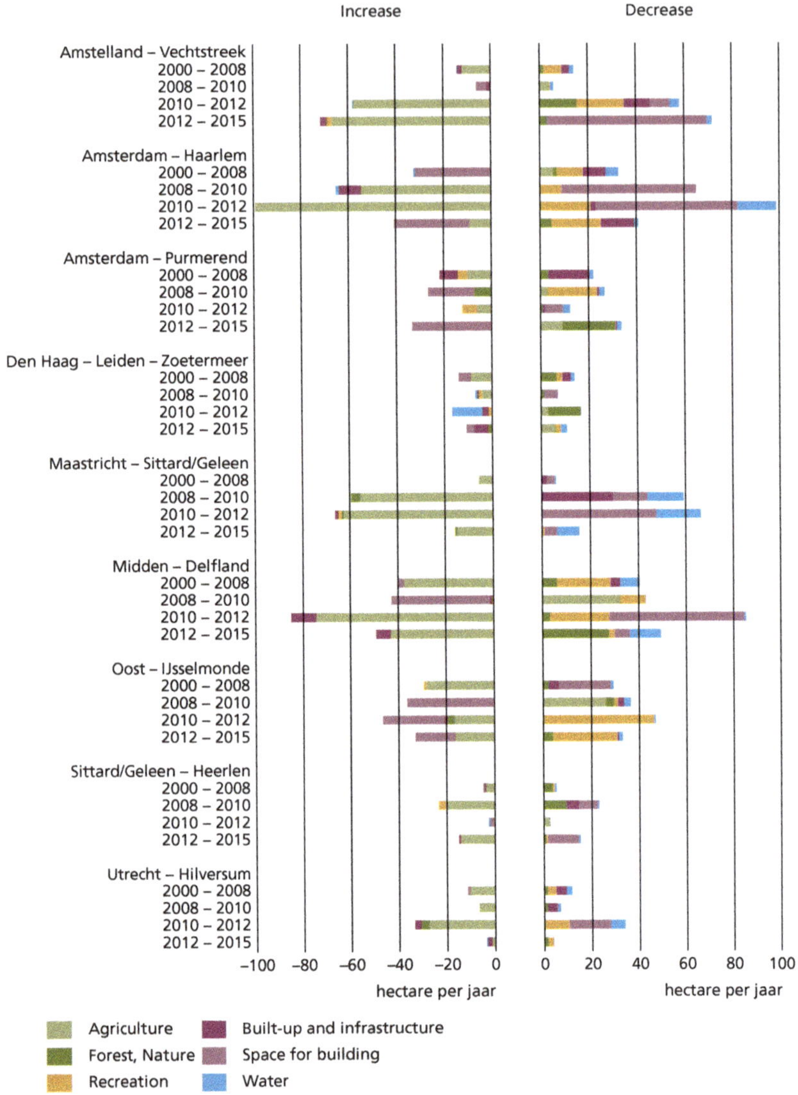

Source: Compendium voor de Leefomgeving. *Verstedelijking, Ontwikkelingen in Rijksbufferzones, 2000–17*, 2018.

Hoofdstructuur (EHS), or ecological main structure, and has the purpose of safeguarding biodiversity and nature in the Netherlands. The main objective is to maintain, recover and develop natural landscapes and to balance the role of humans and nature. This ecological network, which was intended to be completed by 2018, now covers about 15 per cent of the country's total rural area,[26] approximately 680,000 hectares.

A major driver of spatial planning in the Netherlands is the scarcity of space; there is high pressure on every square metre of land in the country. As a result, every layer of government concentrates on optimising the allocation of spatial land uses in such a way that a just and fair assessment of interests can be made. Should a certain use, such as nature, come under pressure, it will be carefully assessed in the spatial planning process at all three levels of government.

In the 1990s greater emphasis was placed on the importance of biodiversity and natural landscapes. The traditional strength of Dutch thinking on landscape architecture is that it pays attention to the systemic properties of green structures, water and ecology. These are seen as a coherent system that should be designed as a separate layer. The Ecological Main Structure (EHS) analyses the Dutch landscape under three categories; core areas, nature development zones and ecological connections. Within the core areas are nature reserves, country estates, forests, large water areas and large agricultural cultural landscapes, with a minimum size of 250 hectares. Nature development constitutes the second layer. These zones are areas with significant ecological development potential of national or international importance. Ecological connections, the third layer, are meant to connect core areas and development areas with each other.[27]

This large connected system of nature aims to:

- Allow more space for natural processes and ecological diversity
- Offer more species a suitable habitat – the minimal size guaranteeing sustainable populations
- Fine tune environmental and water conditions so the requirements of nature can be better safeguarded[28]

For every part of the EHS, ecological goals are formulated, consisting of a specific, measurable, ecological qualitative objective. The broader ambition is now to connect the EHS to ecological connection zones and nature reserves in neighbouring countries.

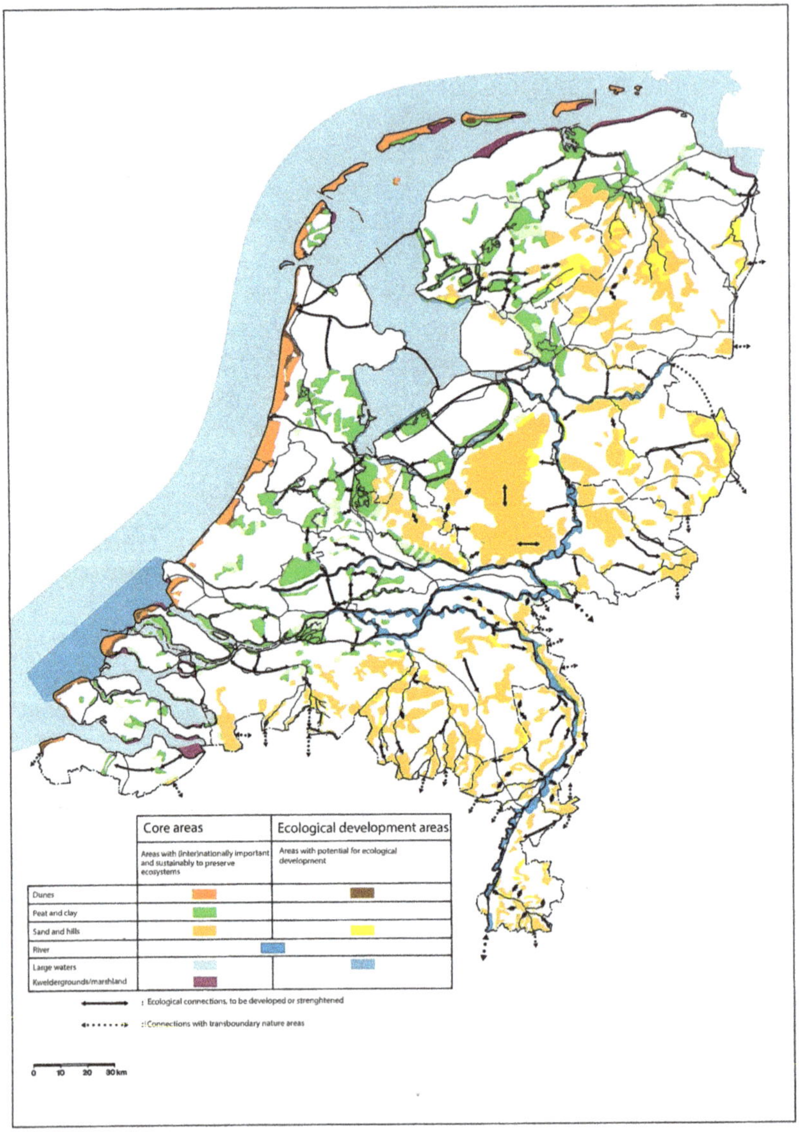

Fig. 4.4 Map showing the *Ecologische Hoofdstructuur* (Ecological Main Structure of the Netherlands), 1990.

Source: Ministerie van Landbouw, Natuurbeheer en Visserij. *Natuurbeleidsplan*. Den Haag: Ministerie van LNV, 1990.

Casco-planning and the strategy of the two networks

Water boards have traditionally had a strong role in the democratic process in the Netherlands. Ever since the 12th century[29] the fight against the water has united people and urged them to collaborate on planning and water management, in particular the draining and protection of the land for all its inhabitants. This concern has fundamentally influenced the focus of the Dutch landscape architecture school, which has used this systemic approach to water management as the basis for much of its theoretical and practical teaching. This approach has also embraced water quality and the relationship of this to land use. In the 1970s water in the Netherlands was of poor quality due to intensive agricultural practices. In order to address this problem, its causes were systemically researched and the contributory factors and different components analysed using separate layers of landscape. This eventually led to the development of the Casco-concept.

In understanding the ecology of the water system, soil and nature become important factors in an integrated approach to landscape and spatial planning. This is reflected in concepts that use layers to analyse different spatial elements. Based on the work of McHarg,[30] this 'layer-approach' is widely used in the Netherlands.[31] This analytical instrument distinguishes an abiotic, a biotic and an anthropogenic layer which when integrated shape the landscape. This concept is also used in policy making and planning. Since 2001 the Dutch national government has used this approach to identify planning opportunities, using different layers: subsoil, networks and occupation. It assumes that occupation patterns are nested in the infrastructure networks, which are in turn embedded in the substrate system.[32] The layers aim to separate different dynamics of use. Under this thinking the subsoil is seen as changing extremely slowly, the networks change at a moderate pace and the occupation patterns can change relatively rapidly.

The Casco-concept is a spatial manifestation of how these different spatial dynamics are separated.[33] The lower dynamics in the landscape, such as nature and water, form the Casco, within which higher dynamic uses, such as agriculture, find their space. For urban areas a similar concept is developed. Here the 'two networks strategy' links higher dynamic uses (traffic, industries, intensive forms of agriculture) to the transportation network and the lower dynamic uses (nature, green, water, residential) to the water network.[34] These types of concepts are used to design urban and rural plans and to plan the location of different land uses.

When applied in practice this approach has been used to separate different uses, firstly to design a coherent system of low-dynamic functions in which public green space, water and nature are connected. Within this network utility functions such as the storage of water and the purification of household water are planned. Secondly, the high-dynamic land use functions are planned in a separate network linked to a core infrastructure system. This system should interfere as little as possible with the low-dynamic network and be planned to be far away from these vulnerable activities. This dynamic network consists of (heavy) industry, major road and rail infrastructure, intensive forms of agriculture, ports and energy plants. In a final step residential areas are planned in between the higher and lower dynamic networks to provide a perfect intermediary. These areas receive products such as energy and food at the same time as being accessible through the lower level transport systems. On the other side residential areas are connected with nature and water reserves to organise easy access for leisure. The system also allows for waste be recycled.

'Urban metabolism'[35] describes the city in flows; the concept aims to reduce the use of resources in order to process them as efficiently as possible and to reduce the waste flows. Hence when the city is able to close the cycles within its boundaries, a sustainable situation is achieved. Less resources are extracted from nature and the environment, which in turn remain untouched; less waste is generated and less waste is put back into the environment. This prevents degradation of natural systems and increases their quality, which in turn improves the capacity to restore and deliver renewable resources.

In employing this system, the design of cities focuses on the understanding of networks and flows. These are in turn then based on ways in which the depletion of resources and production of waste are reduced. This allows resources to be reused and recycled within the city (Fig. 4.6). Several studies within urban areas by Nature Biennale[36] have shown how to design the flows in a city, for example the study for Rotterdam.[37] In this study nine flows have been analysed and quantified at the regional and local scale (Goods, People, Waste, Biota (for example, movements of plants and animals), Energy, Food, Fresh Water, Sand and Clay and finally Air). The question of how 'urban metabolism' can contribute to increased sustainability in the development of the city was addressed in 2010 by Kennedy et al.[38] He makes a case that studies urban material flows and the ways in which these should be integrated into the designs made by architects, engineers and planners for the metabolism of a sustainable city.

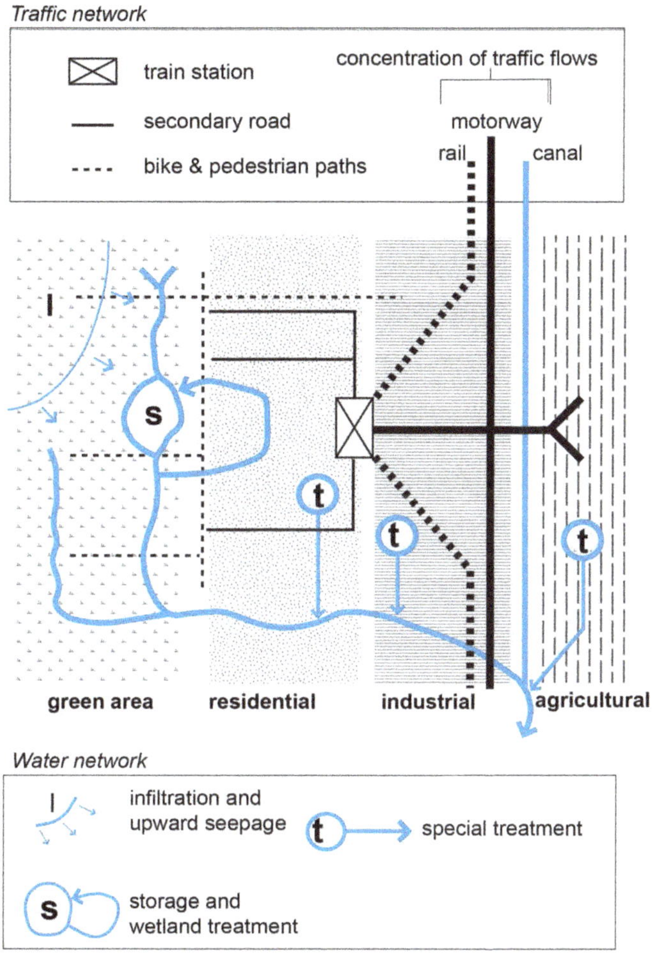

Fig. 4.5 Diagram showing the 'Two Networks Strategy', 1995.

Source: Tjallingii, S.P. *Ecopolis: Strategies for ecologically sound urban development*. Leiden: Backhuys Publishers, 1995.

Designing the city on the basis of its urban metabolism requires shifting between regional and local scales, between strategic design and spatial design and between flows and the associated infrastructure. Four integrated strategies couple economic, ecological and spatial diversification with a comprehensive reading of city, nature, and landscape.[39] In the first strategy, 'Collecting Resources', raw materials are obtained from waste and food, such as aquafarming or phosphate recovery. In the

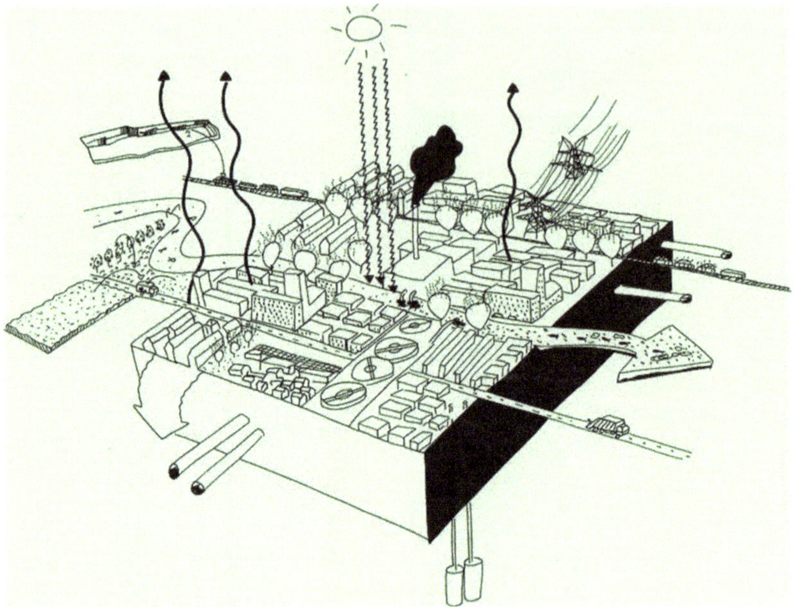

Fig. 4.6 Technical diagram of the Urban Metabolism Model, 2014.

Source: Sijmons, D. and Raith, J. 'H+N+S Landschapsarchitecten', *IABR 2014 – Urban by Nature*, edited by G. Brugmans and J. Strien. Amsterdam: Idea Books, 2014.

second strategy, 'Urban Biotopes', urban nature is improved by locally sourced fresh water, sand and clay, and an ecological energy network and water landscapes to be planned. In the third, 'Channelling (energy) Waste', by-products of energy extraction are collected – including organic carbon dioxide, used for the assimilation of plants – to establish heat hubs in the city. The fourth strategy, 'Catalysing Re-industrialisation', addresses the flows of goods and people. It considers how these might be made more efficient through the introduction of regional public transport rings and knowledge axes.

All these policies, except for the urban metabolism model (never adopted as a formal national policy), have been abandoned over the last decade. The reasons for this are complex, but are mainly due to a neo-liberal policy shift in the Dutch planning processes which has led to the abandonment of land uses that are not immediately profitable. Increasingly all plans are required to deliver a positive land exploitation (financial return). Even in the municipality of Almere – where the land has always been owned by the national government and where, in theory at least, future land use can be planned in a balanced way to optimise social and environmental returns, there has been a move away from the comprehensive landscape plans and spatial planning approaches embodied by the Casco system. In earlier phases of development it was possible to keep green zones between urban cores open and to plan for buffer zones simply by not selling the land for urban development. Recently, even in Almere City, the green and water system previously safeguarded under the local plan has shrunk due to financial and exploitation pressure.

This is characteristic of what is happening elsewhere in the Netherlands. The power of the municipal land bank department and project developers enables them to pursue higher profits at the cost of weaker land use functions, namely those that cannot generate a financial return. As low-dynamic functions cannot easily be monetarised, they often lose the battle for space. This has led to marginalised plans in which the space for greenery, ecology and water is reduced. In Almere less green space is being provided in the newer urban neighbourhoods. In most other Dutch cities agricultural land is bought by developers as soon as new development locations are planned by the national government. The result of this speculative process has been apparent in neighbourhoods in which densities have gone up at the expense of space for the 'softer' uses that has reduced.

Nevertheless, the planning of green systems at both regional and national level has generally been successful in keeping green space open in between cities, in maintaining ecological quality, in promoting uses such as leisure, in maintaining water management and in preserving other 'soft' uses. Moreover the policy is popular, as people appreciate the landscape next to their urban environment.

What is interesting about the Dutch approach is the fact that, dating back to the 1950s, the preservation of open countryside has not been part of a pursuit of an arcadian idyll: it is rather embedded as a sense of a natural environment possessing a deeply symbiotic relationship to the city. The countryside in the Netherlands is not an abstract concept, but is rooted in the struggle between the Dutch and their fragile and vulnerable landscapes. Crucially the landscape in Holland is not a natural construct: it has been wrested from the sea. As such it is a resource to be managed and reshaped according to need. Land scarcity, water management and ecology are set deep within planning policy in a way that is unique to the Netherlands and was well ahead of its time. Could these concepts – originally adopted from the Green Belt concept and developed in the Dutch context – be brought back to the UK and there offer new insights to rejuvenate Green Belts? In this way the UK could re-import

Green Belt thinking, improved and adapted in other contexts, and make the policy fit to face the challenges of the 21st century.

Rejuvenated landscapes

One of the options for giving neglected green and open spaces new meaning is to allow them to play a role in rejuvenating landscapes. Climate change, sea level rises and flood risk are adding new imperatives to the debate. In recent years the Dutch policy in dealing with flood risk has changed from a responsive approach to an adaptive one. Near flooding of some of the country's large rivers (the River Maas in 1993 and 1995, the River Waal in 1995) resulted in a major evacuation of a large part of the river area. This has led to different national policies being established. One of them, literally the 'Space for the River' programme,[40] emphasised that rivers require more space to behave in a natural way in order to reduce flood risk. In recent years the broadening of riverways has taken place to allow for natural water storage and release.[41] Specific programmes have also been started to create 'green rivers'. These seek to open up green spaces to accommodate any surplus discharging water, to establish overflow areas for the temporary storage of water next to the rivers and to strengthen the network of dykes and dams.

All of these programmes were a combination of spatial design, water management and an extensive engagement process. Not only has this extra space given rivers more room to accommodate flood dynamics, but it has also been part of a deliberate process to naturalise the fluvial environment and regenerate the river system ecologically. This way of thinking is based in concepts such as self-organisation and emergence that allow us to deal with uncertainty and change by designing interventions as specific dynamic inputs for urban and rural environments.[42] If the landscape is seen as an adaptive system, it opens avenues for an easier adjustment to (sudden) changes; this in turn increases the system's resilience. This also means that the landscape is capable of a faster and easier natural reorganisation without the intervention of man. Consequently, if we can understand how the system organises itself, potential interventions can be designed that work with it; such processes of self-organisation can also indirectly increase resilience. These concepts are common in nature and can be used to make future cities and landscapes more adaptable.[43] The design for a climate-proof Groningen,[44] a province in the northern Netherlands, or the plan for the Sand Engine,[45] for instance, are good examples of building with nature.[46] In short, this approach allows nature to self-adapt because natural, landscape forming processes have the power to enhance resilience.

In the plan for a climate-proof Groningen, the space for these natural processes has been extended (Fig. 4.7). It turns out that in a normal planning process, the actual spatial changes that are allowed to occur are limited to around 2 per cent over a 15-year period.[47] However, for a landscape to be adaptive, around 30 per cent of the land use should possess such potential. In particular, more space for nature and water storage is required, while agriculture should be adapted from a centralised, large-scale system to a localised and saline one.[48] When the space for these changes is made, landscape (and urban) systems have the

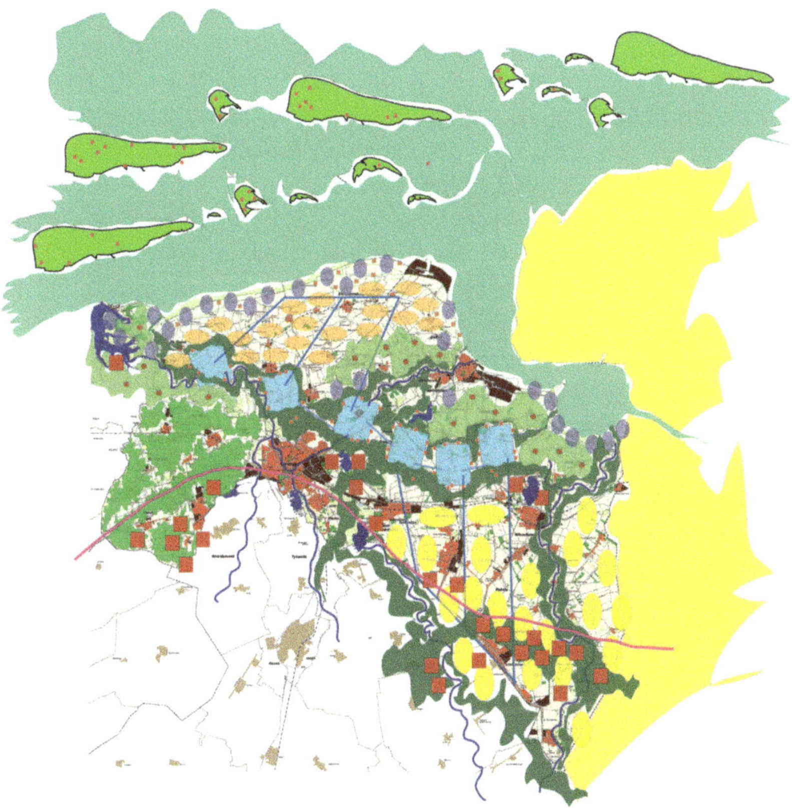

Fig. 4.7 Landscape plan for an adaptive Groningen province, 2012.

Source: Roggema, R. *Swarm Planning: The development of a spatial planning methodology to deal with climate adaptation*. PhD thesis. Delft: Delft University of Technology, 2012.

freedom to self-organise and adjust themselves to future demands and requirements.

The Sand Engine is based on similar principles. Every season the coastline of the Netherlands needs to be reinforced with large amounts of sand to safeguard its beaches and, more importantly, to protect its coasts and the hinterland. The Sand Engine plan anticipates the power nature offers in the form of currents, waves and wind. By supplying sand to the coastal sea, nature itself will bring it to the coast and produce sandbanks, beaches and dunes in a natural way. In this way a natural system of coastal protection emerges which is stronger than any artificial solution and saves considerable costs and effort. The results of this self-organising landscape approach are promising and seem to work as planned.[49]

Interventions such as the examples described above are not uncommon in the Netherlands. There is a strong, design-led culture to create future land forms, driven by the nature of the low-lying land and the threats of flooding. As changes in climate become more pressing, this spirit kindles very long-term planning that fundamentally rethinks the very shape and topography of the country.

For a long time the Dutch counted on their engineering skills to deal with the sea. However, the predicted acceleration in sea-level rise has forced a rethink of practice and new avenues for protecting the country are being considered. In the early 2000s the consequences of extensive sea-level rise were already being thought through. This early concept plan[50] shows a country in which the majority of the population has retreated to higher ground, with low-lying marshland replacing the current urban agglomerations. This gives space for water storage and natural saline landscapes which in turn naturally protect the higher grounds from flooding. As an extra layer of safety, the country would also extend further into the sea through a protective row of barrier islands in front of the current coastline (Fig. 4.8). In the same spirit, a plan for a second row of barrier islands north of the current Wadden Sea has been proposed.[51]

In 2019 several publications pointed to a gap in Dutch planning strategies for dealing with future extreme events, such as the impact of Antarctic ice loss on the Dutch coastal protection strategy[52] and the increasing risks of changes in the Greenland ice sheet.[53] The Netherlands now needs to have a 'Plan B' to respond to sea levels rising faster than expected.[54] Given that 50 per cent of the Netherlands is vulnerable to sea and river flooding, this concern has given rise to renewed attention to long-term,

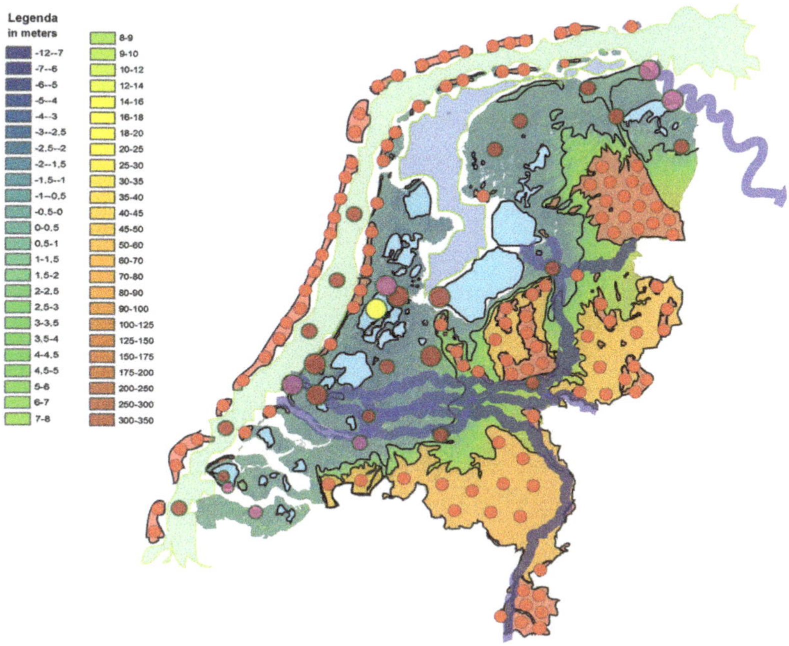

Fig. 4.8 Plan showing the Netherlands in an imagined future of 2150, under the influence of strong climate change. First Dutch Adaptation Map, 2007.

Source: Roggema, R. *Ruimtelijke impact adaptatie aan klimaatverandering in Groningen*. Groningen: Provincie Groningen, 2007.

anticipative planning and design at the national level. Responses have primarily been instigated from within the landscape architecture community. The design office LOLA have produced their 'Plan B'.[55] In this vision the low-lying parts of the country are returned to the sea, protected by a small but firm row of connected dunes, safeguarding the existing conurbations like bastions from the Middle Ages. Meanwhile the majority of the population has retreated beyond this new coastline to higher ground (Fig. 4.10).

The Blauwe Kamer, a Dutch professional magazine on landscape architecture and urbanism, responded to LOLA's work with an open invitation for practices to formulate their own plan B.[56] This resulted in a new wave of visionary statements, spatial solutions and vistas, which can roughly be subdivided into groups of attackers, land consolidators, radical poets and fatalists. These visions and plans illustrate the capability of Dutch

Fig. 4.9 Map showing a second row of barrier islands to protect the northern part of the Netherlands, 2006.

Source: Roggema et al. *Pallet of Possibilities*. Groningen: Grounds for Change, 2006.

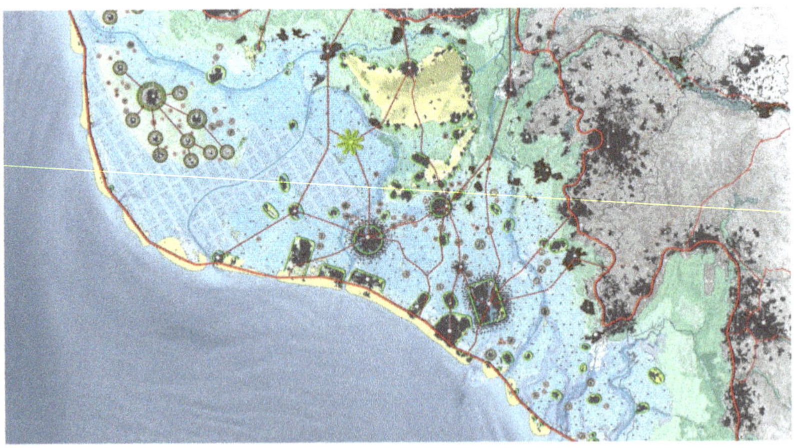

Fig. 4.10 Plan B for the Netherlands in an imagined future of 2200, 2019.

Source: LOLA Landscape Architecten. *Plan B, Nederland 2200*, 2019.

designers to think outside the box and to use the landscape, man-made in the first place, to turn the threat of extreme climate change into a positive vision for future living. This way of using landscape strategies to keep the Netherlands alive is extraordinary. It shows the determination of the Dutch to sustain their position in the danger zone.

Letting nature do its work, however, needs to address two ways of current thinking. The first concerns institutional inertia – the use of tried and tested solutions, regardless of whether the requirements have changed. The persistent use of path-dependency, for example, often leads to the repetition of old solutions for problems that have changed. For example, we respond to increased storm surge by building higher dykes, as we have done for as long as we can remember. Instead of lowering the risk, however, this increases the chance of an unforeseen disaster: if the dyke breaks unexpectedly, the surge of water is huge and overwhelming. We need to use our imagination and to think in counterintuitive ways,[57] as this is the only way in which unprecedented futures can be assessed, and radical responses developed that deal with uncertainty. It cannot be assumed that existing solutions will work in an uncertain future.

Secondly, in striving for technical solutions, rigid and fixed approaches do not give us options for future adaptation, whereas increasing spatial flexibility might. In a city where the surrounding landscape is part of the urban planning process, spatial voids are a designed-in redundancy; they could thus provide the space to accommodate future uses that cannot be known at the time of planning.[58] Thinking in unorthodox ways and creating spatial flexibility gives natural processes the time and space to create resilience. This could invest degraded Green Belts with a new meaning and role.

New demands on the landscape

Aside from new adaptive approaches to landscape, open green space can also play a role in accommodating new demands – programmes that require space that were not priorities before now. In particular, the need for sustainable local and regional resources could impact significantly on emerging spatial policy. The need for renewable energy sources, the growth of locally sourced food and the sustainable management of water flows are novel claims on the regional landscape. Yet these could provide an opportunity to use existing left-over green spaces within the Green Heart and buffer zones for different purposes.

Such new demands are being implemented in green open spaces in different ways to respond to different demands. New uses for the peri-urban landscape can shape the green policy spatial framework of urbanised regions and give Green Belts new meaning in the following ways:

a. Local food production close to cities results in productive landscapes that are able to connect the production, transport, preparation and consumption of food.[59] In addition, it is possible to link water and energy supply to these systems at a regional scale, as has already been illustrated for the Amsterdam urban landscape.[60] This has benefits including healthier food, fresher food, fewer food miles and growth environments that are easier to control. When the 'New Diet', a balanced and sustainable food regime that uses locally sourced produce,[61] is used to shape these landscapes, these foodscapes will create locally oriented, sustainable, climate resilient and healthy landscapes. In the Groningen province the first experiments with these foodscapes are under way, providing healthy produce for local restaurant chefs.[62] Locally sourced food based on the Dutch climate, production environment and culture are being used to provide new diets. Figure 4.11 shows the balance of ingredients that might reduce consumption of meat, fats, sugar and wheat in favour of beans, vegetables and fruit. The local urban hinterland can provide a broad range of suitable ingredients to generate a healthy and sustainable diet.
b. The potential of the landscape to generate energy from renewable resources is underused and seldom analysed or taken into consideration. For the northern Netherlands an Energy Potential Mapping (EPM) study has been carried out (Fig. 4.12). This investigates the various renewable sources that could become available for the generation of electricity and heat.[63] The potential for sustainable energy production is leading planning policy to rethink specific land uses and has provided the conditions for landscape planning based on renewable energy typologies. Scientists and regional policy-makers have calculated that the province of Groningen could provide more than sufficient energy to supply the current needs of all residents, industries and other uses (Fig. 4.12).[64]
c. In the Netherlands especially, but also in many other countries, climate change will lead to short-term surpluses of water followed by longer-term shortages. Until recently the surpluses were discharged into the sea as quickly as possible, but drought is now increasingly impacting on the landscape, its ecology and agriculture. Retaining

water though sophisticated, landscape-based water management systems could mitigate against these processes and partly offset the impacts of climate change. Climate 'buffers'[65] operate as a type of sponge, absorbing water and so buffering its impact for a while, then releasing it slowly. In this way they can store excess water for a time while also enhancing local nature development and biodiversity. The De Onlanden project (Fig. 4.13), in the northern provinces of

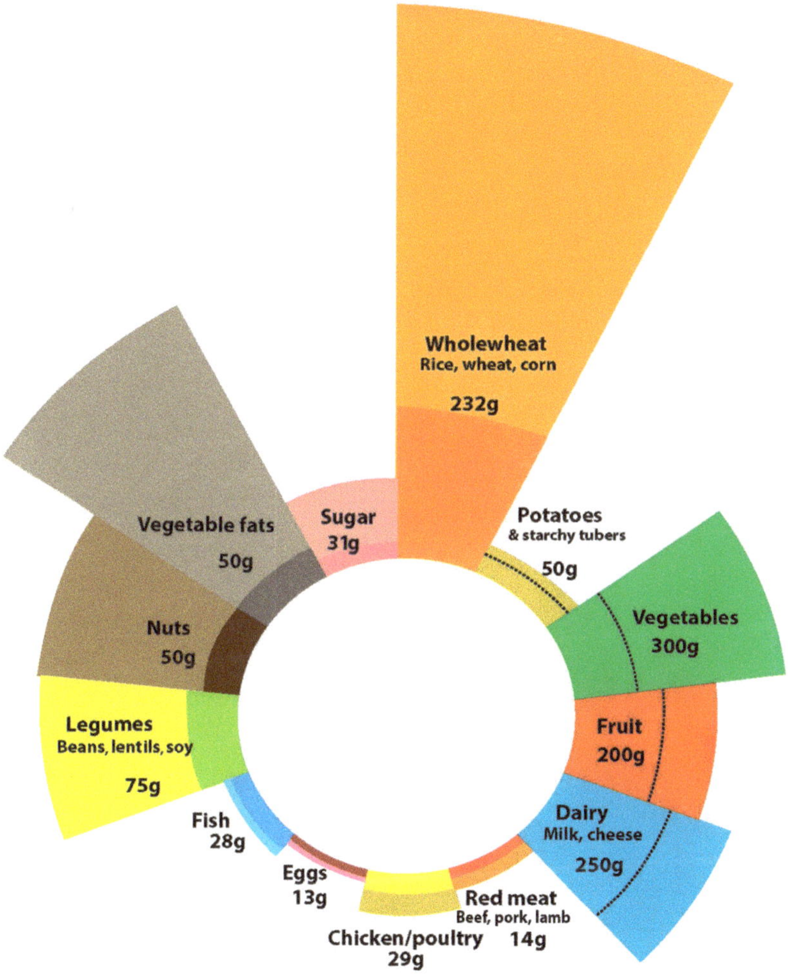

Fig. 4.11 Chart showing Dutch localised amounts of food according to the New Diet, 2019.

Source: Roggema, R. *ReciproCity: Giving instead of taking*. Inaugural lecture. Groningen: Hanze University of Applied Sciences, 2019.

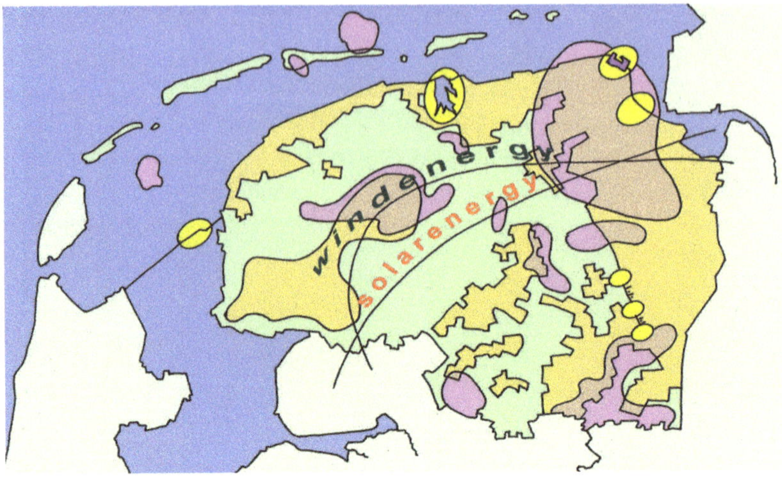

Fig. 4.12 Diagram showing future energy potential for the northern part of the Netherlands, 2010.

Source: Roggema et al. 'Groningen Fast Forward: Towards a fossil-free region in 2050'. In *Proceedings, 'IRE 2010'*. Hanoi, 2010.

Fig. 4.13 Map showing the creation of space for storing water: 'Wet Nature for Dry Feet'.

Source: Stichting Kop van Drenthe (unpublished).

Fig. 4.14 Photograph of De Onlanden, 2016.

Source: Photograph by Jurjen Veerman.

> the Netherlands, has demonstrated how water retention and storage strategies can utilise flexible green space to deal with sudden rainfall fluctuations on a regional scale. Moreover it has led to a landscape (Fig. 4.14) that is diverse and ecologically rich, and is highly appreciated by local residents and visitors alike.

These examples represent three domains of conceptual thought and action which combine to offer new thinking on the function of regional landscapes. They could give these Green Belt or in-between green and open landscapes a new meaning and purpose. This is the essence of the Food–Energy–Water–Nexus[66] that aims spatially to integrate these domains. This moveable nexus represents a basis for innovative thinking[67] that takes a design-led approach to minimise the impact of food, energy and water systems by reducing their footprint and integrating systems flows at different scales. The linkage between design, engagement and appraisal is a key component of this thinking and can lead to fruitful and feasible spatial propositions. It also allows the carbon footprint of different strategies to be calculated. Current uses (diet, energy and water use) are first charted, then translated into carbon dioxide (CO_2) equivalents and recalculated as the area of forest required to compensate these uses. Once this is understood, a range of design options can be investigated to reduce space utilisation; these can then be integrated into new spatial propositions. This integrated way of working optimises resource provision and can be translated into programmes that engage local stakeholders in responsible decision making. Green spaces are thus developing a new role in becoming productive and beneficial for the local population.

'Beltscape'

When taking an historic perspective, the morphology of urbanisation can be subdivided into three periods (Fig. 4.15). For a long time the city had a clear border, the city wall, that marked the line between what was inside and outside.[68] Urban density was clearly located inside the walls, while the outside landscape was either an empty wilderness or used to grow food. Although spatially defined, the city was functionally dependent on its

Fig. 4.15 Illustration showing three stages of urbanisation: the compact city; the sprawling city; the 'Beltscape'.

Source: The author.

rural hinterland for food, fuel, water and building materials. Prosperous cities were generally located within prosperous regions.

When the walls were no longer necessary, cities expanded rapidly. The centres were still the densest places, often with higher rise districts, but they became surrounded by residential neighbourhoods that eventually sprawled on the urban fringes until the open countryside was finally reached. The urban countryside was viewed by many as the 'yet to be developed city'. At the same time the rise of regional and international transportation and distribution systems meant that a clear relationship between the city and its region could become diluted. This ongoing urbanisation has continued to take place. Many conurbations face endless suburban neighbourhoods with low densities; they are dependent on car mobility and consequently have serious environmental problems such as air pollution.

A third period is now under way. In this the city has become so extensive that distances are too great and sub-centres need to be developed for culture, leisure and shopping. The limitations of proximity to raw materials, food and energy have been broken by transport systems based on cheap (and non-renewable) energy, and the city no longer has an inter-dependency with its hinterland. For many cities in the world this rapid process has been poorly thought through, resulting in a low-density, single use urban form with no planned mix of green or public spaces. Moreover these areas, despite being enormous in size, are often of extremely low density.

However, the pressures of scarce land, climate change, water management, renewable energy and food security, along with urban resilience, may now be ushering in a new era. The city is no longer a defined entity, but is rather a regional possibility of different scales, densities and land uses. There is no need to fill up the gaps in between existing hubs with urban sprawl. By turning the thinking on its head, could the landscape offer specific areas where dense urban hubs, mixed-use residential and commercial areas can be integrated in a planned environment, all with easy and close access to green spaces? Could the gateway to renewed thinking about the Green Belt be the creation of an innovative 'Beltscape'?

When the spatial quality of these urban hubs, populated with large numbers of people, is of the highest quality, the surrounding, in-between landscape can be used for other supportive uses. These include providing space for flood control, for cooling the city, for generating energy, for regenerating water, for growing food and for the enhancement of degraded ecological systems. In addition, these new types of Green Belts could also fulfil their original purpose of offering a recreational resource for the city. Could this landscape offer space for people to take time to think, reflect and replenish?[69] Could it become a place in which the hectic pace of urban life and the pressures of urban living can be relieved? A consciously planned and designed 'Beltscape' would complement the buzz of the city with the tranquillity of a rewilded landscape.

Such a 'Beltscape' would consist of several functions:

- A new, high-quality, spatial landscape. The current disengagement of planning at the regional scale exacerbates the ongoing degradation of the quality of green open landscapes. In the 'Beltscape' the boundaries between green and urban would be more precisely defined and the fringe would become an area that has been consciously designed. In other words, the fringe is transformed from a void lacking qualities into a real place
- A new typology of urban landscape in which separation of urban and rural is no longer the objective, but instead provides a well-balanced spatial relationship between high-density hubs in the landscape and a regenerated countryside. Through integrated regional design, the city is planned in association with its landscape
- Accommodation of new productive uses, such as the cleaning and storage of water, increased biodiversity, the generation of energy from renewable sources and the growing and processing of food
- The space to accommodate climate change and climatic hazards. Within a resilient landscape spaces may be planned in which floodwater can temporarily be stored and green and forest areas planted to help decrease heat and provide water in prolonged drought periods
- Transformation of urban and green spaces. When urban ecology in the form of new parks and connected green public spaces replaces parts of the current built urban form, more condensed urban uses can partly be allocated within the broader landscape and the overall quality of the 'Beltscape' improves. Swapping land use allocations in this way has been common practice in rural areas in the Netherlands, in the so-called Ruilverkaveling[70]

'Beltscape' design principles

Planning for the 'Beltscape' requires a new approach from the regulatory frameworks that led to the establishment of the Green Belt. The following design principles can be applied to enhance the qualities of these areas:

1. Design the landscape and city as an integrated regional system, leaving behind the traditional dichotomy of urban–rural
2. Interchange 'red' (urban areas) and 'green' (countryside areas) to enhance the ecological and cooling qualities inside urban precincts and to increase the urbanity of rural areas
3. Introduce redundant space, or voids, in the landscape to create the space for unplannable climatic hazards
4. Include local productive uses such as cleaning and storage of water, increased biodiversity, generation of energy from renewable sources and the growing and processing of regional food
5. Transform unusable areas into productive, resource-delivering, sustainable areas

Conclusions

This chapter has illustrated ways in which the original Green Belt concept has been adapted and used in the Dutch planning system. Initially it separated green and red uses and safeguarded green spaces in urban landscapes. Later the concept was transformed creatively to accommodate new claims, uncertain futures and create greater landscape flexibility as part of strategies to improve resilience to climate change. There is scope for this thinking to be re-introduced in the UK to give Green Belts new and contemporary meaning.

One of the major problems of Green Belts is they have been planned from a regulatory perspective – that is, planning to determine where development could be built and where it could not. A spatial vision or a regional design has long been absent in UK thinking, as has any policy that specifically concerns itself with the function and intrinsic quality of the Green Belt. In the absence of these structures, the Green Belt has been eroded both spatially and qualitatively. An alternative, learning from the Netherlands, would be to develop regional plans in which the landscape is taken as the point of departure, in which the risks and vulnerabilities are transformed into ecological and resilience programmes.

Green Belts have a range of benefits which are key to sustainable planning at the regional level:

- They are a huge unplanned space that can be used for different spatial strategies when needed in the future
- They are capable of generating energy locally from renewable sources, growing food, cleaning and storing water. The Green Belt is not an

empty void: it is a resource that can provide for waste recycling, energy production and the production of products for local consumption. It is a *sustainable* zone and should be valued accordingly

- Green Belts create lower temperatures through their vegetation and water-rich environments. These are capable of mitigating heat waves and are able to cool the land
- Green Belts are ecosystems, containing rich biodiversity and ecology. They provide important complementary space for the urban population to recreate, exercise, enjoy the fresh air and the green surroundings

To grasp these opportunities a new spatial concept is proposed: the 'Beltscape'. The design principles for developing 'Beltscapes' are to rethink the red (city) and green (countryside) areas in order to increase the overall quality of both. This will create spaces for unplannable future claims that will turn disadvantages and unusable areas into new spatial opportunities. Dutch planning is based on the long traditions of a country that has literally created its own landscape. Landscape in the Netherlands is not concerned with some kind of bucolic nostalgia that has to be preserved. The Dutch landscape is a man-made construct, and as such has its own dynamics. It has been moulded and adapted; the Dutch have developed a methodology for doing this in order to adapt to an uncertain future. These concepts could be extended to other countries and cities as they strive to cope with climate change over the course of this century.

Notes

1. Tummers and Tummers-Zuurmond 1997, 111.
2. College van Rijksadviseurs 2019.
3. Abercrombie 1944.
4. Tummers and Tummers-Zuurmond 1997.
5. Ministerie van Landbouw, Natuurbeheer en Visserij 1990.
6. Ministerie van Volkshuisvesting en Bouwnijverheid 1960.
7. Werkcommissie Westen des Lands 1958.
8. Ministerie van Volkshuisvesting en Bouwnijverheid 1960.
9. Verstedelijkingsnota, part of the Third National Plan on Spatial Policy, Ministerie van Volkshuisvesting en Ruimtelijke Ordening 1977.
10. Ministerie van Volkshuisvesting, Ruimtelijke Ordening en Milieubeheer 1988.
11. Ministerie van Volkshuisvesting, Ruimtelijke Ordening en Milieubeheer 1991.
12. The Green Structure of the Randstad, Ministerie van Landbouw, Natuurbeheer en Visserij en Ministerie van Volkshuisvesting, Ruimtelijke Ordening en Milieubeheer 1995.
13. Bervaes et al. 2001.
14. Ministerie van VROM 2001.
15. Bervaes et al. 2001; Van der Wouden 2015.
16. Faludi and Van der Valk 1996.

17. Faludi and Van der Valk 1994.
18. Burke 1966.
19. Ministerie van Volkshuisvesting en Bouwnijverheid 1960.
20. Kooij 2006.
21. Van der Cammen and Witsen 1995.
22. Fazal et al. 2012.
23. Lambrechts et al. 2006; Lambrechts 2009.
24. Roggema w. De Plaa 2009.
25. Ministerie van Landbouw, Natuurbeheer en Visserij 1990.
26. Jongeneel et al. 2008.
27. Geurs 2002.
28. Van Hinsberg 2004.
29. Van der Woud 1987.
30. McHarg 1969.
31. Van Schaick and Klaasen 2011.
32. Priemus 2007.
33. Sijmons 1992.
34. Tjallingii 1995; 2015, fig. 4.5.
35. Wolman 1965; Newman 1999; Kennedy et al. 2007; Kennedy et al. 2010; Shafiea et al. 2013.
36. Brugmans and Strien 2014.
37. Tillie et al. 2014.
38. Kennedy et al. 2010.
39. Tillie et al. 2014.
40. Programmabureau Ruimte voor de Rivier 2016.
41. Q-team Ruimte voor de Rivier 2012; Programmabureau Ruimte voor de Rivier 2016; Sijmons et al. 2017.
42. Portugali, 2000; Roggema 2012.
43. Waterman 2010.
44. Roggema 2009a.
45. Stive et al. 2013.
46. Waterman 2010.
47. Roggema 2012.
48. Roggema 2009a.
49. Luijendijk and Van Oudenhoven 2019.
50. Roggema 2007.
51. Roggema 2007.
52. Haasnoot et al. 2019.
53. Shepherd et al. 2020.
54. Schuttenhelm 2019.
55. LOLA 2019.
56. https://www.blauwekamerezine.nl/ezine-2019-8/.
57. Roggema 2019a.
58. Roggema 2018.
59. Roggema and Keeffe 2014.
60. Roggema and Spangenberg 2015.
61. Willett et al. 2019.
62. Roggema and Van Spijk 2019.
63. Roggema and Van den Dobbelsteen 2005; Schoot Uiterkamp et al. 2005; Van den Dobbelsteen et al. 2006; Van den Dobbelsteen et al. 2007a; 2007b; 2008; Roggema et al. 2009; Roggema et al. 2010.
64. Roggema 2009b.
65. Litjens et al. 2006; Andriesse et al. 2007; Smit et al. 2014; Eurosite undated.
66. Yan and Roggema 2019.
67. www.m-nex.net.
68. Touropia.
69. Roggema 2019b.
70. Molema and Brink 2009.

References

Abercrombie, P. *Greater London Plan, 1944*. London: University of London Press, 1944.

Andriesse, L.A., Akkerman, G.J., Van den Broek, T., Vos, P., Martens, D.C.A.M., Stroeken, P.F.A. and Speets, R. *Natuurlijke klimaatbuffers voor een klimaatbestendiger Nederland*. Rotterdam: Royal Haskoning Netherlands, 2007.

Bervaes, J.C.A.M., Kuindersma, W. and Onderstal, J. *Rijksbufferzones, Verleden, heden en toekomst*. Wageningen: Alterra, Research Instituut voor de Groene Ruimte, Alterra-rapport 360, 2001.

Brugmans, G. and Strien, J., eds. *IABR 2014 – Urban By Nature*. Amsterdam: Idea Books, 2014.

Burke, G.L. *Greenheart Metropolis. Planning the Western Netherlands*. New York: St Martin's Press, 1966.

CBS, PBL, RIVM, WUR. *Ontwikkelingen in Rijksbufferzones, 2000–2017*, 2018 (indicator 2010, versie 07, 6 september 2018). http://www.clo.nl. Centraal Bureau voor de Statistiek (CBS), Den Haag; Planbureau voor de Leefomgeving (PBL), Den Haag; Rijksinstituut voor Volksgezondheid en Milieu (RIVM), Bilthoven; and Wageningen University and Research (WUR), Wageningen. Accessed 30 January 2020.

College van Rijksadviseurs. *(X)XL–Verdozing. Minder, compacter, geconcentreertder, multifunctioneler*. Den Haag: Cra, 2019.

Compendium voor de Leefomgeving. *Verstedelijking, Ontwikkelingen in Rijksbufferzones, 2000–2017*, 2018. https://www.clo.nl/indicatoren/nl2010-ontwikkelingen-in-rijksbufferzones. Accessed 25 January 2020.

Eurosite. *Defining Natural Climate Buffers*, no date. https://www.klimaatbuffers.nl/uploads/eurosite-ncb-leaflet-v04-a4.4aa3cb.pdf. Accessed 3 December 2019.

Faludi, A. and Van der Valk, A.J. *Rule and Order: Dutch planning doctrine in the twentieth century*. Dordrecht: Kluwer Academie Publishers, 1994.

Faludi, A. and Van der Valk, A. 'The Green Heart Debate', *Tijdschrift voor Economische en Sociale Geografie* 87 (5) (1996): 448–57.

Fazal, S., Geertman, S.C.M. and Toppen, F.J. 'Interpretation of Trends in Land Transformations – A case of Green Heart region (The Netherlands)', *Natural Resources* 3 (2012): 107–17. http://dx.doi.org/10.4236/nr.2012.33015.

Geurs, K. *Ontsnippering van natuurgebieden: effecten op natuur, mobiliteit, bereikbaarheid, verkeersveiligheid en geluid*. Bilthoven: RIVM, 2002.

Haasnoot, M., Kwadijk, J., Van Alphen, J., Le Bars, D., Van den Hurk, B., Diermanse, F., Van der Spek, A., Oude Essink, G., Delsman, J. and Mens, M. 'Adaptation to Uncertain Sea-Level Rise: How uncertainty in Antarctic mass–loss impacts the coastal adaptation strategy of the Netherlands', *Environmental Research Letters* 15 (3) (2019). https://doi.org/10.1088/1748-9326/ab666c.

Jongeneel, R., Polman, N. and Slangen, L. 'Cost-benefit Analysis of the Dutch Nature Conservation Policy: Direct, indirect effects and transaction costs of the ecological main structure in the Netherlands'. In *Proceedings, 12th Congress of the European Association of Agricultural Economists – EAAE*. Ghent, 26–29 August 2008.

Kennedy, C., Cuddihy, J. and Engel-Yan, J. 'The Changing Metabolism of Cities', *Journal of Industrial Ecology* 11 (2) (2007): 43–59.

Kennedy, C., Pincetl, S. and Bunje, P. 'The Study of Urban Metabolism and Its Applications to Urban Planning and Design', *Environmental Pollution* 159 (8–9) (2010): 1965–73.

Kooij, P. 'Hoe ons Nederland een groen hart kreeg en het ook weer verloor', *Bijdragen en Mededelingen betreffende de Geschiedenis der Nederlanden* 121 (4) (2006): 753–70.

Koomen, E., Dekkers, J. and Van Dijk, T. 'Open-Space Preservation in the Netherlands: Planning, practice and prospects', *Land Use Policy* 25 (3) (2008): 361–77. https://doi.org/10.1016/j.landusepol.2007.09.004.

Lambrechts, B. *The Polycentric Metropolis Unpacked: Concepts, trends and policy in the Randstad Holland*. Amsterdam: Amsterdam Institute for Metropolitan and International Development Studies (AMIDSt), 2009.

Lambrechts, B., Kloosterman, R., Van der Werff, M., Röling, R. and Kapoen, L. 'Randstad Holland: Multiple Faces of a Polycentric Role Model'. In *The Polycentric Metropolis – Learning from mega-city regions in Europe*, edited by P. Hall and K. Pain, 137–45. London: Earthscan, 2006.

Litjens, G., Van den Herik, K.J., Van Winden, A. and Braakhekke, W. *Natuurlijke klimaatbuffers. Adaptatie aan klimaatverandering, wetlands als waarborg*. Nijmegen: Stroming B.V., 2006. In

opdracht van: Vereniging Natuurmonumenten, Vogelbescherming, Waddenvereniging, ARK en Staatsbosbeheer.
LOLA Landscape Architecten. *Plan B, Nederland 2200*, 2019. https://twitter.com/LOLA_=landscape/status/1115993012591525888/photo/1.
Luijendijk, A. and Van Oudenhoven, A., eds. *The Sand Motor: A nature-based response to climate change: findings and reflections of the Interdisciplinary Research Program NatureCoast*. Delft: Delft University Publishers – TU Delft Library, 2019.
McHarg, I.L. *Design with Nature*. New York: Natural History Press, 1969.
Ministerie van Landbouw, Natuurbeheer en Visserij. *Natuurbeleidsplan*. Den Haag: Ministerie van LNV, 1990.
Ministerie van Landbouw, Natuurbeheer en Visserij en Ministerie van Volkshuisvesting, Ruimtelijke Ordening en Milieubeheer. *Structuurschema Groene Ruimte*. Den Haag: Ministerie van LNV, 1995.
Ministerie van Volkshuisvesting en Bouwnijverheid. *Nota inzake de Ruimtelijke Ordening in Nederland*. Den Haag: Ministerie van V&B, 1960.
Ministerie van Volkshuisvesting en Ruimtelijke Ordening. *Derde Nota over de Ruimtelijke Ordening – Deel 2, Verstedelijkingsnota*. Den Haag: Ministerie van VRO, 1977.
Ministerie van Volkshuisvesting en Ruimtelijke Ordening en Milieubeheer. *Vierde Nota Ruimtelijke Ordening*. Den Haag: Ministerie van VROM, 1988.
Ministerie van Volkshuisvesting en Ruimtelijke Ordening en Milieubeheer. *Vierde Nota Ruimtelijke Ordening Extra (VINEX-Nota)*. Den Haag: Ministerie van VROM, 1991.
Ministerie van Volkshuisvesting, Ruimtelijke Ordening en Milieubeheer. *Ruimte maken, ruimte delen, Vijfde Nota Ruimtelijke Ordening*. Den Haag: Ministerie van VROM, 2001.
Molema, A.M. and Brink, A. 'In naam van het algemeen belang: De ontstaansgeschiedenis van de ruilverkaveling als instrument voor inrichting van het platteland', *Tijdschrift voor Geschiedenis* 122 (1) (2009): 72–85.
Newman, P.W.G. 'Sustainability and Cities: Extending the metabolism model', *Landscape & Urban Planning* 44 (1999): 219–26. https://doi.org/10.1016/S0169-2046(99)00009-2.
Portugali, J. *Self-Organisation and the City*. Berlin: Springer, 2000.
Priemus, H. 'The Network Approach: Dutch spatial planning between substratum and infrastructure networks', *European Planning Studies* 15 (5) (2007): 667–86.
Programmabureau Ruimte voor de Rivier. *Ruimte voor de Rivier in 8 thema's. Longreads Ruimte voor de Rivier*. Utrecht: Programmabureau Ruimte voor de Rivier, 2016.
Q-team Ruimte voor de Rivier. *Jaarverslag 2009–2010–2011 Kwa/iteitsteam Ruimte voor de Rivier*. Utrecht: Programmadirectie Ruimte voor de Rivier, 2012.
Roggema, R. *Ruimtelijke impact adaptatie aan klimaatverandering in Groningen*. Groningen: Provincie Groningen, 2007.
Roggema, R. *DESIGN: Final report hotspot climate-proof Groningen*. Groningen/Amsterdam: Province of Groningen and Climate Changes Spatial Planning, 2009a.
Roggema, R., ed. 'INCREASE II (International Conference on Renewable Energy Approaches for the Spatial Environment)', 208. In *Proceedings Increase II, Groningen*. Province of Groningen and Beijing: UIBE, 2009b.
Roggema, R. *Swarm Planning: The development of a spatial planning methodology to deal with climate adaptation*. PhD thesis. Delft: Delft University of Technology, 2012.
Roggema, R. 'Design With Voids. How inverted urbanism can increase urban resilience', *Architectural Science Review* 61 (5) (2018): 349–57. Special issue: *Time, Place and Architecture*. https://doi.org/10.1080/00038628.2018.1502153.
Roggema, R. 'The Joy of Counterintuitive-ity'. In *Design for Coastal Resilience*, edited by E. Mossop, 73–92. Boca Raton: CRC Press, 2019a.
Roggema, R. *ReciproCity: Giving instead of taking*. Inaugural lecture. Groningen: Hanze University of Applied Sciences, 2019b.
Roggema, R. w. De Plaa, P. *From the Dutch New Spatial Law via Development Planning towards Swarm Planning: First contours of an emerging new planning paradigm*. Hotspot Climate Proof Groningen. Groningen: Province of Groningen and Climate Changes Spatial Planning, 2009.
Roggema, R. and Keeffe, G., eds. *Why We Need Small Cows: Ways to design for urban agriculture*. Velp: VHL Publishing, 2014.
Roggema, R., Middleton, L. and Van den Dobbelsteen, A. 'Quadruple the Potential'. In *Proceedings, 'PLEA 09'*. Quebec, 21–24 June 2009.

Roggema, R. and Spangenberg, J. 'New Urban Networks for Linking the Urban Food Production–Preparation–Consumption Chain'. In *Proceedings, 51st ISOCARP Conference*. Wageningen, 19–23 October 2015.

Roggema, R. and Van den Dobbelsteen, A. 'Energy-Design for Energy Valley Challenges'. In *Grounds for Change: Bridging energy planning and spatial design strategies*, edited by F. van Dam and K.J. Noorman. Charrette Report, Groningen: Grounds for Change/IGU, 2005.

Roggema, R., Van den Dobbelsteen, A. and Stegenga, K. *Pallet of Possibilities*. Groningen: Grounds for Change, 2006.

Roggema, R., Van den Dobbelsteen, A., Stremke, S. and Mallon, W. 'Groningen Fast Forward: Towards a fossil-free region in 2050'. In *Proceedings, 'IRE 2010'*. Hanoi, 2010.

Roggema, R. and Van Spijk, A. *The Groningen Foodscape: Towards a sustainable and healthy local food system for Groningen province*. KIEM-application. SIA-RAAK, 2019.

Schoot Uiterkamp, T., Van Dam, F., Noorman, K.J. and Roggema, R. 'The Northern Netherlands: Scanning the future'. In *Grounds for Change: Bridging energy planning and spatial design strategies*, edited by F. van Dam and K.-J. Noorman. Charrette Report. Groningen: Grounds for Change/IGU, 2005.

Schuttenhelm, R. 'De zeespiegelstijging is een groter problem dan we denken. En Nederland heeft geen plan B'. *Vrij Nederland*, 7 February 2019. https://www.vn.nl/zeespiegelstijging-plan-b/. Accessed 25 January 2020.

Shafiea, F.A., Dasimah, O. and Karuppannanb, S. 'Urban Metabolism: A research methodology in urban planning and environmental assessment'. In *Proceedings, the 1st International Conference on Research Methodology for Built Environment and Engineering*. Kuala Lumpur, Malaysia, 17–18 December 2013.

Shepherd, A., Ivins, E., Rignot, E. et al. 'Mass Balance of the Greenland Ice Sheet from 1992 to 2018', *Nature* 579 (2020): 233–9. https://doi.org/10.1038/s41586-019-1855-2.

Sijmons , D. *Het casco-concept, een benaderingswijze voor de landschapsplanning*. Utrecht: Ministerie van LNV, directie NBLF, 1992.

Sijmons, D., Feddes, Y., Luiten, E., Feddes, F. et al. *Ruimte voor de Rivier, veilig en mooi landschap*. Wageningen: Uitgeverij Blauwdruk, 2017.

Sijmons, D. and Raith, J. 'H+N+S Landschapsarchitecten'. In *IABR 2014 – Urban by Nature*, edited by G. Brugmans and J. Strien. Amsterdam: Idea Books, 2014.

Smit, M., Oosterhuis, F., Van Kreveld, A. and Braakhekke, W. *De natuur als partner bij klimaatadaptatie. Een procesevaluatie van tien klimaatbufferprojecten*. Den Haag: PBL, 2014.

Stive, M.J.F., De Schipper, M.A., Luijendijk, A.P., Ranasinghe, R.W.M.R.J.B, Van Thiel de Vries, J.S.M., Aarninkhof, S., Van Gelder-Maas, C., De Vries, S., Henriquez, M. and Marx, S. 'The Sand Engine: A solution for vulnerable deltas in the 21st century?' In *Proceedings, Coastal Dynamics 2013: 7th International conference on coastal dynamics*. University of Bordeaux, Arcachon, France, 24–28 June 2013.

Tillie, N., Klijn, O., Frijters, E., Borsboom, J. and Looije, M. *Urban Metabolism Rotterdam*. Rotterdam: IABR and Municipality of Rotterdam, 2014.

Tjallingii, S.P. *Ecopolis: Strategies for ecologically sound urban development*. Leiden: Backhuys Publishers, 1995.

Tjallingii, S. 'Planning with Water and Traffic Networks: Carrying structures of the urban landscape', *Research In Urbanism Series* 3 (1) (2015): 57–80. https://doi.org/10.7480/rius.3.832.

Touropia. '22 Most Impressive Walled Cities in the World', no date. https://www.touropia.com/walled-cities-in-the-world/.

Tummers, L.J.M. and Tummers-Zuurmond, J.M. *Het land in de stad: de stedebouw van de grote agglomeratie*, 148–9. Bussum: THOTH, 1997.

Van den Dobbelsteen, A., Gommans, L. and Roggema, R. 'Smart Vernacular Planning: Sustainable regional design based on local potentials and optimal deployment of the energy chain'. In *Proceedings, 'World Sustainable Building Conference'* (SB08). Melbourne, 21–25 September 2008.

Van den Dobbelsteen, A., Jansen, S., Van Timmeren, A. and Roggema, R. 'Energy Potential Mapping – A systematic approach to sustainable regional planning based on climate change, local potentials and exergy'. In *Proceedings, CIB World Congress*. Cape Town, 14–18 May 2007a.

Van den Dobbelsteen, A.A.J.F., Roggema, R. and Stegenga, K. 'Grounds for Change: The sustainable re-development of a region under threat of climate change and energy depletion'. In *Proceedings, SASBE 2006: 2nd CIB International conference on smart and sustainable built environments*, s.n., ed., 435–42. Shanghai, 15–17 November 2006. Shanghai: CIB / SRIBS, 2006.

Van den Dobbelsteen, A., Roggema, R., Stegenga, K. and Slabbers, S. 'Using the Full Potential: Regional planning based on local potentials and exergy'. In *Management of Natural Resources, Sustainable Development and Ecological Hazards, The Ravage of the Planet I*, edited by C.A. Brebbia, M.E. Conti and E. Tiezzi, 177–86. Southampton: WIT Press, 2007b.

Van der Cammen, H. and Witsen, P.P. *Hartelijke groeten, uit het Groene Hart: Tweeëntwintig vaak gestelde vragen over het Groene Hart-beleid*. Den Haag: Ministerie van Volkshuisvesting, Ruimtelijke Ordening en Milieubeleid, 1995.

Van der Woud, A. *Het Lege Land; De ruimtelijke orde van Nederland 1798–1848*. Amsterdam: Olympus, 1987.

Van der Wouden, R. *De ruimtelijke metamorfose van Nederland 1988–2015. Het tijdperk van de Vierde Nota*. Den Haag/Rotterdam: Nai010/PBL, 2015.

Van Hinsberg, A. *Ecologische hoofdstructuur en het milieu: Achtergronddocument bij natuurbalans 2004*. Wageningen: Natuurplanbureau, 2004.

Van Schaick, J. and Klaasen, I.T. 'The Dutch Layers Approach to Spatial Planning and Design: A fruitful planning tool or a temporary phenomenon?', *European Planning Studies* 19 (10) (2011): 1775–96.

Waterman, R.E. *Integrated Coastal Policy Via Building With Nature*. PhD thesis. Delft: Delft University of Technology, 2010.

Werkcommissie Westen des Lands (Working Committee for the Western Netherlands). *De ontwikkeling van het westen des lands*, deel 1 rapport. Den Haag: Rijksdienst voor het Nationale plan, 1958.

Willett, W., Rockström J., Loken, B., Springmann, M., Lang, T., Vermeulen, S., Garnett, T., Tilman, D., DeClerck, F., Wood, A., Jonell, M., Clark, M., Gorden, L.J., Fanzo, J., Hawkes, C., Zurayk, R., Rivera, J.A., De Vries, W., Sibanda, L.M., Afshin, A., Chaudhary, A., Herrero, M., Augustina, R., Branca, F., Lartey, A., Fan, S., Crona, B., Fox, E., Bignet, V., Troell, M., Lindahl, T., Singh, S., Cornell, S.E., Srinath Reddy, K., Naraïn, S., Nishtar, S. and Murray, C.J.L. 'Food in the Anthropocene: The EAT–*Lancet* Commission on healthy diets from sustainable food systems', *The Lancet Commissions* 393 (10170) (2019): 447–92. https://doi.org/10.1016/S0140-6736(18)31788-4.

Wolman, A. 'The Metabolism of Cities', *Scientific American* 213 (3) (1965): 179–90.

Yan, W. and Roggema, R. 'Developing a Design-led Approach for the Food–Energy–Water Nexus in Cities', *Urban Planning* 4 (1) (2019): 123–38. Special issue: 'The City of Flows'. https//:doi.org/10.17645/up.v4i1.1739.

Chapter 5

Conclusions: the Green Belt – a legacy for the 22nd century

Peter Bishop

The Green Belt is one of the few planning measures in the UK that has entered the public consciousness. Like the NHS it has a universal, widespread appeal and an almost sacred status. 'Green Belt' is a powerful brand name that garners broad support, often without a deep understanding of its role and function. Very few people would argue that urban sprawl is a good thing; most would support policies that preserve the open countryside around our towns and cities. In some ways the very success of the Green Belt 'brand' is part of the problem. It polarises debate into two camps: those that argue for it to remain untouched and those who argue for its partial or total release for development. This makes any debate on the Green Belt both politically contentious and somewhat sterile.

This book has examined the history of the Green Belt from its origins in the UK at the end of the 19th century to the present day, considering changes in its function as well as debates about its future. It has also looked at the Green Belt's adoption in other countries and the impact that it has had on the interrelationship of the city and its regional landscape. Given the radical changes that have occurred over the past century in society, the economy of cities, urban theory and in transport and technology, the resilience of the Green Belt as an 'institution' is remarkable. Yet the growing importance of environmental concerns about ecological degradation, resource depletion and climate change has hardly impacted on the debate on the role and function of Green Belts, at least not in any sophisticated way. A fundamental reappraisal of the Green Belt is thus arguably long overdue, but it should not be driven by issues such as house prices. Such a review should instead ask searching questions about the interconnectivity of cities and their natural hinterlands, about how the growth (even the possible future decline) of cities can be properly planned, about truly sustainable patterns of living and about how the quality of life can be improved, both in the countryside and in the city.

When analysing the Green Belt in the UK it is possible to identify significant changes in its role and purpose. In the 1930s the Green Belt was seen as a mechanism to preserve the open countryside and to make it publicly accessible, particularly to the urban population. In the post-war period Green Belts grew significantly; their express purpose was to restrict urban growth and preserve the amenity of those living in the countryside. In the present era the focus of interest in the Green Belt has been largely dominated by pressures to deliver more housing and accommodate urban growth. The Green Belt risks becoming a commodity – land that has not (yet) been developed. Some believe that if the Green Belt could be released then housing supply would be increased, which would ultimately balance demand and reduce house prices. The temptation to build on Green Belt land is certainly not new, but in the past it has been resisted. In 1969 a report by the GLC clearly restated the importance of the Green Belt:

> A little peripheral building, a belt a mile wide all the way around London … would give us enough housing. This argument fails to realise the cost to all of us … the main effect would be to choke our lines of communication … not only would travel to work become more difficult … but it would become equally more difficult for those living in the city to get out at weekends or holiday times.[1]

When considering the debate about the future of the Green Belt, we should first reflect on what it has achieved. It has undoubtedly contained cities and prevented urban sprawl. Transport congestion around cities in the UK may at times be bad – but had the unrestricted outward growth of suburbia been allowed, it would have been considerably worse. The restrictions on the outward growth of cities have also led to the reuse of brownfield land, and to compact urban forms that are the basis for more sustainable models of living. The Green Belt has safeguarded a belt of open countryside around our cities; some of this has public access, while other areas provide havens for nature and wildlife. It has also meant that a number of towns in the countryside have successfully preserved their individual distinctiveness and character. That said, perhaps the most important aspect of today's Green Belt is that a legacy of open land has been passed down to us from previous generations. They did not squander it for short-term gain: neither should we. It is a precious resource that should be used responsibly and passed on to future generations.

Returning to the original purpose of the Green Belt, the ideal of access to the countryside as a prerequisite to improving the health of urban populations was an enlightened one. So too were the programmes to purchase land (or to secure open access) by bodies such as the National Trust and the London County Council. The original thinking on the Green Belt clearly took place in the context of improving the conditions of urban living; reducing sprawl was secondary.

The Green Belt was originally seen as a relatively narrow green corridor around the city. The introduction of planning controls after the Second World War distorted the original ideals that had led to the Green Belt's creation. Its principle purpose was no longer about access to the countryside, but rather the containment of cities. This effectively created a green place that served the amenity of those fortunate enough to live there. The regressive nature of this policy was compounded when the populations of urban areas began to grow rapidly towards the end of the 20th century.

Many cities across the world have adopted Green Belts in one form or another. These take different forms – from protected parklands at the city edge to encircling Green Belts and environmental buffers. Although the UK model is of a city surrounded by a concentric Green Belt (with or without satellite towns), this is not the only form able to restrict sprawl and preserve the open countryside. Linear urban models, such as those proposed by Arturo Soria for Madrid (chapter 2) and the Five Finger Plan for Copenhagen, also fulfil this purpose; they produce dense urban forms with access to the countryside that can be served by efficient transport systems. In this respect, the proposals put forward by academics at the LSE for growth corridors between London and Cambridge have a clear rationale.[2]

Green Belts can be implemented through planning controls, legal instruments or land purchase. Land purchase is the most effective, but is likely to be prohibitively expensive unless land can be secured at agricultural prices. Where planning mechanisms are the sole instrument, there is clear evidence that the Green Belt is likely to be eroded. This might be a slow process, but it is a relentless one. The UK's pattern of piecemeal review through Local Plans (driven by increasingly onerous housing targets) is not strategic and is patently unable to make rational decisions on the future shape of the city. Such a process is also unable to assess the relative qualities and optimal uses of land within the region as a whole. A random reallocation of land on the city fringe is only likely to produce another unsustainable suburban 'onion ring'. If there is to be an effective debate on the future of the Green Belt, it needs to be coupled with new spatial models of the city and its regional hinterland.

There is currently no strategic planning forum in the UK capable of evaluating options on whether the city should be contained within its existing spatial boundaries (and so become ever more compact and dense), whether it should grow along transport corridors (star-shaped with green 'fingers') or whether there should be a series of compact and connected settlements within an urban field. London's use of Metropolitan Open Land and the All London Green Grid could be seen as a forerunner of a spatial model that 'urbanises' the countryside and 'ruralises' the city. What is indisputable is that the present system of decision making is wholly inadequate.

The present planning system in the UK might be 'plan led', but in practice the process of making Local Plans is lengthy and cumbersome. In addition, the weakness of local planning authorities – especially smaller authorities outside the metropolitan areas – means that the system is increasingly less able to resist development proposals. The resources that developers and landowners can bring to Local Plan Inquiries means that the odds are stacked heavily in favour of Green Belt release. If the complex issues around the Green Belt are to be adequately addressed, there needs to be a shift towards a more proactive planning system that is both strategic and regional.

There is no doubt that we have a crisis in housing delivery in parts of the UK, particularly in London and the South East. There is also little doubt, in theory at least, that the relaxation of planning restrictions on the Green Belt would increase the supply and affordability of housing. The appeal of such an approach depends on one's faith in market economics. There is no guarantee either that the housebuilding industry has the capacity to deliver the level of affordable housing that is needed or that development would take place in the right locations, served by the necessary infrastructure. Arguments for the release of a proportion of land within the Green Belt, especially around transport hubs and on the edges of existing settlements, are more compelling, but they are only adjustments to the planning system. Such arguments also tend to ignore the realities of where affordable housing is actually needed – mostly in the city.

The approach in the 1920s and 1930s to land purchase in the Green Belt was enlightened, but ultimately unsustainable. In today's political climate such programmes would, unfortunately, be considered unrealistic. Yet there is money available. It lies in the land itself, through the huge increases in value conveyed by the granting of planning consent for housing. The Green Belt in the UK is a specifically designated area – a zone that appears in Local Plans and on property records. As such, it would be possible to apply fiscal policies to tax this value uplift or allow local authorities (or special purpose vehicles such as Development Corporations) to acquire land for development at existing use value, through compulsory purchase. Land for development would be selected according to clearly defined criteria and then passed on to developers. The difference between the purchase price and the onward sale value would be retained by the public sector and ringfenced for a variety of defined purposes. These might include the purchase of additional land for recreational or environmental use, subsidies for affordable housing or the building of essential infrastructure. The German planning and land purchase scheme outlined in chapter 2 presents an interesting model that could be developed elsewhere.

Two main conclusions may be drawn from the two case studies on the London urban fringe in chapter 3. The first is that the urban fringe is a complex, transitional zone that extends deep into the town as well as out into the countryside. It should be studied and planned as an entity in its own right. This raises interesting questions around densification of the outer suburbs as well as housing incursions into the Green Belt. The second conclusion is that much of the urban edge that is Green Belt is in fact of mixed value. In the UK and the Netherlands some of this fringe land is occupied by uses such as golf courses, rough grazing, horticulture, camp sites, caravan parks and scrap yards. This is not to say these activities are not important. Such *terrains vague* have a role in their own right, and consequently the zone is worthy of planning consideration to assess how these roles might be optimised.

We are now one-fifth of the way through the twenty-first century, and one of the few certainties is that the scale of climate change will pose significant challenges to many aspects of urban living. One of the key lessons from the Netherlands (chapter 4) is the concept of strategic land management. This recognises that the landscape is a dynamic element, one that requires active management and state intervention to optimise its functionality. Contrast this with the approach in the UK and the poverty of thinking is striking. To see the Green Belt purely in terms of a natural landscape (which it is not) or as land not yet developed is to ignore any notion of its functionality. To base planning decisions primarily on their impact on the local amenity of existing residents is clearly both limited and regressive. Questions around the production of food, the conservation of nature, resource management and the generation of energy should be central themes of a planning debate – not whether housing should be built in a particular place or not.

The difference between the Dutch strategic landscape model and the approach in the UK is in essence one of agency. In the UK the role of planning in the Green Belt has been to *stop* development in order to prevent change to an immutable countryside. The traditions of Dutch planning reach far deeper into the complex nature of landscape and its relationship with natural systems. An *engineered* landscape offers a completely different perspective for spatial thinking. It also ushers in a more sophisticated debate. The landscape is no longer the 'yet to be developed' or the 'must be preserved' of the UK debate around the Green Belt. The Dutch have shown how the spatial relationship between the city and countryside can be combined with models of critical interdependency that transcend arbitrary political and administrative boundaries.

A Green Belt for the 22nd century

Over a century on from its creation, there are compelling arguments for reviewing the Green Belt. These should not, however, be concerned with short-term pressures to accommodate urban growth. Instead they should ask bigger questions regarding the nature of the relationship between the city and its regional landscape, about adaption and resilience to climate change, about social equality and the strategic roles of planning and fiscal management. The Green Belt is a precious resource that should be carefully assessed prior to any alteration, in order to optimise its future use and function.

Away from the urban fringe, much of the designated Green Belt is in agricultural use. Considerable areas have little ecological value and only limited recreational access. Present debates around the future of farming subsidies post-Brexit could usher in subsidies for rewilding, ecological management and increased recreational access. Transformations on this scale will require planning, powers and funding. The following framework is proposed for consideration:

i) A strategically planned approach to the Green Belt should replace the simple red/green delineation of city and countryside. A regional planning mechanism based on cities and their hinterlands should be introduced. These city regions should assess their needs in terms of housing, energy, water management, transport, etc., and plan accordingly.
ii) Such a planned approach should be based on detailed survey and appraisal of the Green Belt to assess its intrinsic quality on a

hierarchy of nature conservation and ecology, water management, heritage protection, recreation, productive agriculture/horticulture, energy production and supportive infrastructures, including waste and recycling.

iii) The scale of this survey work suggests that it should be prioritised according to broad spatial models. There are strong arguments in favour of urban growth along designated transport corridors. This might even result in an extension of the Green Belt over a wider area.

iv) Once completed, remaining land should be considered for development *if there are insufficient* brownfield options available and where there is access to spare infrastructure capacity. New housing developments should be compact and at a minimum density of 90 houses per hectare (to support a sustainable community).

v) Primary legislation should be brought in to allow public authorities to acquire land at close to existing agricultural values and pass it on for development. This should be backed up by a betterment tax on private development.

vi) The value uplift captured should be reinvested in acquiring agricultural and other open land for nature conservation, afforestation and public access. There would be an assumption of a significant quantitative and qualitative net gain from this process. Other calls on funds would include improving infrastructure, purchasing and ameliorating brownfield land and subsidising affordable housing and open space provision in urban areas.

vii) The regional planning authorities would be required to provide annual environmental audits of their areas.

Underlying this model is the experience of the Netherlands. A Green Belt that is restructured to meet long-term environmental sustainability criteria could play a critical role in creating liveable cities and addressing climate change. Such an approach would be interventionist and would take environmental management, rather than planning, as its reference point. This represents a significant challenge to the ways in which we think about cities in the UK. If we are unwilling to embrace these challenges and fundamentally change our approach, then perhaps we should leave the Green Belt intact for future and hopefully more responsible generations.

Notes

1. GLC 1969.
2. Mace et al. 2018.

References

Greater London Council (GLC). *Tomorrow's London. A background to the Greater London Development Plan*. County Hall, London, 1969.

Mace, A., Blanc, F. and Mossa, A. 'The London Cambridge Corridor – Making more of Green Belt', London: LSE with Levitt-Bernstein, February 2018.

Index

www.ingramcontent.com/pod-product-compliance
Lightning Source LLC
LaVergne TN
LVHW052018300826
846742LV00020B/86

* 9 7 8 1 7 8 7 3 5 8 8 5 0 *